FATHER MARQUETTE'S JOURNAL

A *Michigan History Magazine* Heritage Publication

Michigan Historical Center, Michigan Department of State
Lansing, Michigan
1998

Other heritage publications from
Michigan History Magazine:

Michigan Soldiers in the Civil War
When the Railroad Was King
Subject Guide to Michigan History Magazine, *1978-1994*
No Tears In Heaven
Michigan and the Civil War: An Anthology

Visit *Michigan History Magazine* and its growing family of heritage publications on the World Wide Web:
www.sos.state.mi.us/history/mag/mag.html

Father Marquette's Journal
Second Edition
ISBN 0-935719-55-5

First published 1990

Printed on recycled paper.
This product was not printed at Michigan taxpayer expense.
OTS-590 (rev. 9/98)

Michigan Department of State
Candice S. Miller, Secretary of State

Contents

Father Jacques Marquette

by James H. Schultz

Into the uncharted wilderness that would be Michigan came the French: Etienne Brulé in 1610, Jean Nicolet in 1634, Father Claude Allouez in 1665, Robert La Salle in 1679, Antoine Cadillac in 1694. Among these famous explorers and missionaries, one name stands alone as the symbol of contact between the first European settlers and the Native Americans—Father Jacques Marquette.

A Jesuit-educated aristocrat, Marquette chose to minister in the North American wilderness instead of saying Mass in French cathedrals. He preferred the danger of traveling the Great Lakes in a birchbark canoe to the safety of a comfortable teaching position at a French university.

From his arrival in Canada in 1666, until his death in 1675, Marquette accomplished more than most people do in a lifetime. His years in the Great Lakes wilderness inspired legends of his compassion and his zeal to explore.

Legends About Father Marquette

The most popular story about Father Jacques Marquette is that he discovered the Mississippi River. Paintings and monuments reinforce the myth of the Jesuit scholar traveling into unknown territory and discovering North America's greatest river for European civilization.

Did Marquette discover the Mississippi River? Certainly, the Indians knew of the river. It is possible that major sections of the Mississippi were found independently by various European explorers during the same time period. Marquette's journal indicates that Spain already had a settlement at the mouth of the Mississippi. Marquette may not have discovered the great river, but his journey proved the existence of water routes to the fabled Mississippi.

Another popular Marquette legend is that the missionary spoke six Indian languages. In his journal Marquette stated, "At first, we had to speak by signs, because none of [the Indians] understood the six languages which I spoke." Marquette biographer Father Claude Dablon compared Marquette to St. Francis Xavier, noting, "He resembled that great saint... in the variety of barbarian languages which he mastered."

The Algonquin and the Iroquois languages are as dissimilar as Russian and English. Mastering six Indian languages would have been possible, but difficult. It is more likely that Marquette and Dablon were referring to Indian dialects. Jesuit records of the period state that "Marquette was supposed to learn some of the Algonquin dialects before everything else." This indicates that his prowess in native dialects was considered sufficient for him to begin active missionary life among the Algonquin tribes dwelling around Lake Superior. According to one twentieth-century Jesuit scholar, "the North American Jesuits had made up their minds that the only way to convert the Indians was through the medium of their own language."

Accounts of Marquette's mastery of several Indian languages are still found in books today. But even if Marquette did not know six Indian languages, his knowledge of their dialects was superior to that of many missionaries and traders, and as a translator he was an asset to any wilderness journey.

Adding to the Marquette mystique is the fact that no one knows what he really looked like. No drawing, sketch or painting remains from the period in which he lived. The imagination and skill of painters and sculptors—all reflecting the attitudes of their respective times—provide the only references to his physical stature and facial expressions.

How Marquette achieved this legendary status as an explorer and missionary is a lesson in historical documentation. The real explorers and discoverers of the French colonial era—the voyageurs, the *coureurs de bois* and the Indians—left few written records. The Jesuit missionaries, on the other hand, kept detailed journals. In New France these journals were sent to Quebec each autumn to be edited and published in annual reports chronicling the relations of the Jesuit missionaries and the Indians of North America.

Between 1611 and 1673 the *Jesuit Relations* were published in France by Sebastien Cramoisy. The *Relations* were both a narrative and a fund-raising document. They were popular reading throughout France—especially in the courts of Paris—among wealthy sympathizers to the Jesuit cause in New France. The *Relations* dropped into obscurity as the Jesuits fell out of political power. In 1858 the Canadian government reissued the Cramoisy series of the *Relations* and included Marquette's journal and the two additional sections in this book. Marquette's journal, like the entire *Relations*, offers a unique view of the discoveries, explorations and conditions in North America during the seventeenth century.

Finally, it is easy to attribute legendary characteristics to the men of that era. There is a romance that stirs the imagination. The thought of

12 voyageurs, paddling 35-foot-long canoes loaded with thousands of pounds of furs through uncharted waterways and facing exciting new challenges around every bend, gives a larger-than-life quality to this chapter in Michigan history.

Marquette's Journey

Where does Marquette the legend end and Marquette the man begin? The sixth child of aristocrat Sieur Nicholas Marquette, Jacques Marquette was born in Laon, France, on June 1, 1637. The younger Marquette was called to the priesthood at an early age, and on October 7, 1654, he was admitted to the Jesuit novitiate at Nancy. The social upheaval of the sixteenth century—the Protestant Reformation—had challenged major tenets of the Roman Catholic Church. To counter the Protestant movement, Ignatius Loyola founded the Society of Jesus (known as Jesuits) in 1534 to establish missions throughout the world. The thought of missionary work excited the young Marquette's imagination.

France participated in Europe's competition to explore, conquer and settle new lands for the glory of God and the profit of the monarchy. Marquette wanted to be a part of this.

In May 1666 an eager 29-year-old Marquette arrived in Quebec for assignment to his first mission. He was assigned to the settlement of Three Rivers, about 80 miles west of Quebec. Here, Marquette received practical training in living among the Indians and in day-to-day survival in New France. He became acclimated to the rugged North American forests, the native foods and canoe travel. He also mastered several dialects of the Algonquin language under the tutelage of Father Gabriel Druillettes.

In 1668, Marquette was sent to Sault Ste. Marie with Brother Louis Boeme. Together they founded a mission there and built a chapel for the Chippewa and Ottawa. The area's abundant fishing attracted many Indian tribes and gave Marquette the opportunity to improve his language skills.

Marquette's first two years in New France were spent under the guidance of experienced Jesuits. The formal training period ended in 1669, when Marquette was assigned to the mission of St. Esprit, near another Indian fishing haven—Chequamegon Bay (an area near present-day Ashland, Wisconsin). Marquette was sent to relieve Father Claude Allouez, who had requested a transfer from the mission, feeling he was unsuccessful in bringing Christianity to the Indians. After living among them for two winters, Allouez confessed that "he found it necessary constantly to entreat God to grant him patience for the cheerful endurance of contempt, mockery, importunity and insolence from these barbarians." After Allouez transferred, Marquette managed the mission independently. This was his first real test as a Jesuit missionary.

Although Marquette achieved limited success in converting the Indians of St. Esprit to Christianity, events in 1671 at Chequamegon Bay changed his life forever. In return for aiding a sick Indian, Marquette was given a slave from the Illinois tribe. The slave taught Marquette the Illinois language and told him of the Mississippi River and its potential as a route to a southern or western sea. Influenced by the stories of the river and the slave's interest in Christianity, Marquette committed himself to establishing a mission in the Illinois country.

His plans to travel to the Mississippi River and to the Illinois Indians were delayed by the interplay between the Huron, Ottawa and Ojibwa Indians of Chequamegon Bay and the Sioux. After several Indians from Chequamegon Bay killed a Sioux, they decided to abandon the area to avoid a war. The Huron and Ottawa migrated toward the Sault, and Marquette accompanied them. In the spring of 1671 the Ottawa settled at Manitoulin Island; Marquette followed the Huron to the Straits of Mackinac.

They first settled on Mackinac Island, but soon moved to the mainland. There, in late 1671, Marquette established his second mission and named it St. Ignace, after St. Ignatius Loyola. With its unique location, St. Ignace—which included a chapel and a Huron village—prospered as a stopping place for fur traders to restock their canoes with supplies before proceeding to Sault Ste. Marie or Green Bay.

Within five years, Marquette founded two missions and served in three others. But his greatest experience came in 1672, when he was chosen to accompany Louis Jolliet on a journey to explore the Mississippi River. His knowledge of Indian dialects and his friendship with Superior General Father Dablon probably led to the appointment. This three-month journey in a birchbark canoe with Jolliet would dominate Marquette's life and define his legacy.

Who was Louis Jolliet? Born on September 21, 1645, in Quebec, Jolliet began his education at the Jesuit college there. When he was nine years old, he was accepted into the seminary, but withdrew in 1667. In that same year, Jolliet visited France. But he soon returned to Quebec and undertook a career as a trader and explorer.

Jolliet's reputation as a skilled voyageur, as well as his religious background, made him an ideal leader for the Mississippi expedition.

The governor of New France, Count Louis de Frontenac, noted, "I have deemed it expedient for the service to send the Sieur Jolliet to discover the south sea... and the great river Mississippi, which is believed to empty into the California Sea. He is a man of experience in this kind of discovery."

Jolliet spent the winter of 1672-73 at St. Ignace preparing for the expedition. Using Indians and French traders as their sources of information, Marquette and Jolliet made a map showing the approximate route from St. Ignace to the upper Mississippi River. They gathered food, supplies, gifts for the Indians and paper and ink to record their observations and discoveries. Ninety-pound packs of supplies—the minimum weight a voyageur carried during a portage—were placed in two canoes large enough to carry the seven-man crew.

In France, Marquette's range of travel was limited to walking and riding distances. On the American continent, men could easily travel thousands of miles in one summer season. The birchbark canoe and the network of rivers offered great mobility, unequaled until the advent of the automobile and paved highways. Marquette's frame of reference for daily travel changed from steps to leagues. However, his journal shows that he still counted steps during long canoe portages.

Marquette was the spiritual leader of the Mississippi expedition. Although he served as a translator for Jolliet, his primary purpose was to convert Indian tribes to Christianity. Jolliet was the leader of the five other voyageurs and represented the commercial interests of France. Both Marquette and Jolliet looked for areas of potential economic development, future settlement, mining and fur trading. Both men also were eager to learn where the Mississippi River led, especially since France was still seeking a river that flowed west to California and beyond to the Orient.

The text of Marquette's journal presented in this publication is based on a translation of the *Relations* from *The Jesuit Relations and Allied Documents* by Reuben G. Thwaites, published in 1902. The authorship of the journal has been disputed by scholars for the past century.

Part One of the journal, which begins in St. Ignace on May 17, 1673 is assumed to be written by Marquette and edited by Dablon. It consists of ten sections written in the first person and attributed to Marquette. The titles are in the third person and are probably a later addition by Dablon to make the journal more readable. The majority of Marquette's writings detail the exciting journey down the Mississippi River to the Arkansas River and offer a brief outline of the return trip to Green Bay.

The crew traveled from St. Ignace along the shore of Lake Michigan to Green Bay. Here, Marquette noted the rise and fall of the tides, and the Folle Avoine tribe warned the explorers of a huge river inhabited by demons, monsters and Indians who would "break their heads." Stopping briefly at the St. Francis Xavier mission, the expedition traveled west down the Fox River. The tribe of the Fire Nation provided guides for the portage to the Wisconsin River. Marquette noted that, for the first time, they were traveling on waters that did not flow toward Quebec—a major turning point for the explorers.

On June 17, 1673, the expedition entered the Mississippi River. A week later footprints were discovered on the river's edge. In one of the journal's more dramatic moments, Marquette and Jolliet follow the footprints into the wilderness, leaving the five voyageurs to guard the two canoes. Marquette had found the Illinois he sought. His visit was highlighted by an eloquent speech of an Illinois elder, "How beautiful the sun is, O Frenchman when thou comest to visit us." It is here that Marquette received a calumet to ward off danger.

As the two canoes journeyed further down the Mississippi, the men encountered a huge monster painted on a rock and a powerful "demon" whirlpool where the great river met with the Missouri River. As the explorers traveled south of the Ohio River, real monsters took hold of them—mosquitoes so fierce that the men draped themselves with their canoe sails for protection.

The party encountered two unfriendly Indian tribes. One tribe possessed guns, indicating Spanish contact. Each time the canoes approached the shore, Marquette held the calumet high. The Indians responded peacefully and the canoes landed in relative safety.

On July 17, 1673, the decision was made to begin the journey back to Green Bay. The main concerns were the possibilities of being captured by the Spanish and losing the valuable notes and maps of the journey. Section Ten of the journal gives a brief account of the trip back, including the obvious difficulty of paddling a canoe upstream. Despite this, Marquette retained his enthusiasm, noting the fertile land and abundant wildlife. As the explorers followed the Illinois River to Lake Michigan, they discovered a second canoe route to the east, which would be important to future traders and settlers. The party encountered another Illinois tribe at Kaskaskia and Marquette vowed to return to establish a mission there. The explorers reached Green Bay in September 1673. They had traveled more than 2,500 miles since they had left St. Ignace five months earlier.

Part Two of this publication begins in the summer of 1674 and consists of Marquette's unfinished journal and notes by Dablon. Although Marquette was sick with a serious stomach disorder, he was driven to establish a mission in Kaskaskia. The tone of the account is dominated by the hardships of sickness, travel and winter camp. The winter of 1674 was spent in a small camp at present-day Chicago. By April 1675, Marquette and his two voyageurs were ready to journey to Kaskaskia.

Part Three of this publication is written by Dablon. In his journal we observe a sick, but inspired, Marquette—Marquette the missionary, not Marquette the explorer. In Kaskaskia, Marquette established La Conception, his last mission. We also learn of the circumstances of Marquette's death on May 18, 1675, and his reburial in 1677. The end of the journal clearly demonstrates Marquette's love of his fellow man and the strength of his religious beliefs. It also communicates the love and respect that the French and Indians had for Marquette.

To the present-day reader, Marquette's and Dablon's writings provide a window to the past that reveals many attitudes and beliefs unique to the French colonial era. They also disclose feelings and emotions that bridge more than three centuries—allowing us to see Marquette the seventeenth-century man beyond Marquette the twentieth-century legend.

The journal presented here is little changed from the 1902 English translation by Reuben G. Thwaites in *The Jesuit Relations and Allied Documents*. The original spelling and punctuation have been retained; only capitalization has been changed to allow easier reading. The journal's original subtitles introduce each of this book's chapters. The attitudes and language of the journal—including the use of the term "savages" for North American Indians—are strictly those of the seventeenth century.

Departure of Father Jacques Marquette for the Discovery of the Great River Called by the Savages Missisipi, Which Leads to New Mexico.

PART ONE • SECTION ONE

The Feast of the Immaculate Conception of the Blessed Virgin—whom I have always invoked since I have been in this country of the Outaouacs, to obtain from God the grace of being able to visit the nations who dwell along the Missisipi River—was precisely the day on which Monsieur Jollyet arrived with orders from Monsieur the Count de Frontenac, our governor, and Monsieur Talon, our intendant, to accomplish this discovery with me. I was all the more delighted at this good news, since I saw that my plans were about to be accomplished; and since I found myself in the blessed necessity of exposing my life for the salvation of all these peoples, and especially of the Ilinois, who had very urgently entreated me, when I was at the point of St. Esprit, to carry the word of God to their country.

We were not long in preparing all our equipment, although we were about to begin a voyage, the duration of which we could not foresee. Indian corn, with some smoked meat, constituted all our provisions; with these we embarked—Monsieur Jollyet and myself, with 5 men—in 2 bark canoes, fully resolved to do and suffer everything for so glorious an undertaking.

Accordingly, on the 17th day of May 1673, we started from the mission of St. Ignace at Michilimakinac, where I then was. The joy that we felt at being selected for this expedition animated our courage, and rendered the labor of paddling from morning to night agreeable to us. And because we were going to seek unknown countries, we took every precaution in our power, so that, if our undertaking were hazardous, it should not be foolhardy. To that end, we obtained all the information that we could from the savages who had frequented those regions; and we even traced out from their reports a map of the whole of that new country; on it we indicated the rivers which we were to navigate, the names of the peoples and of the places through which we were to pass, the course of the great river, and the direction we were to follow when we reached it.

Above all, I placed our voyage under the protection of the Blessed Virgin Immaculate, promising her that, if she granted us the favor of discovering the great river, I would give it the name of the Conception, and that I would also make the first mission that I should establish among those new peoples, bear the same name. This I have actually done, among the Ilinois.

THE FATHER VISITS, IN PASSING, THE TRIBES OF THE FOLLE AVOINE. WHAT THAT FOLLE AVOINE IS. HE ENTERS THE BAY DES PUANTS; SOME PARTICULARS ABOUT THAT BAY. HE ARRIVES AMONG THE FIRE NATION.

PART ONE • SECTION TWO

With all these precautions, we joyfully plied our paddles on a portion of Lake Huron, on that of the Illinois and on the Bay des Puants.

The first nation that we came to was that of the Folle Avoine. I entered their river, to go and visit these peoples to whom we have preached the Gospel for several years, in consequence of which, there are several good Christians among them.

The wild oat, whose name they bear because it is found in their country, is a sort of grass, which grows naturally in the small rivers with muddy bottoms and in swampy places. It greatly resembles the wild oats that grow amid our wheat. The ears grow upon hollow stems, jointed at intervals; they emerge from the water about the month of June, and continue growing until they rise about two feet above it. The grain is not larger than that of our oats, but it is twice as long, and the meal therefrom is much more abundant. The savages gather and prepare it for food as follows. In the month of September, which is the suitable time for the harvest, they go in canoes through these fields of wild oats; they shake its ears into the canoe, on both sides, as they pass through. The grain falls out easily, if it be ripe, and they obtain their supply In a short time. But, in order to clean it from the straw, and to remove it from a husk in which it is enclosed, they dry it in the smoke, upon a wooden grating, under which they maintain a slow fire for some days. When the oats are thoroughly dry, they put them in a skin made into a bag, thrust it into a hole dug in the ground for this purpose, and tread it with their feet—so long and so vigorously that the grain separates from the straw, and is very easily winnowed. After this, they pound it to reduce it to flour,—or even, without pounding it, they boil it in water, and season it with fat. Cooked in this fashion, the wild oats have almost as delicate a taste as rice has when no better seasoning is added.

I told these peoples of the Folle Avoine of my design to go and discover those remote nations, in order to teach them the mysteries of our holy religion. They were greatly surprised to hear it, and did their best to dissuade me. They represented to me that I would meet nations who never show mercy to strangers, but break their heads without any cause; and that war was kindled between various peoples who dwelt upon our route, which exposed us to the further manifest danger of being killed by the bands of warriors who are ever in the field. They also said that the great river was very dangerous, when one does not know the difficult places; that it was full of horrible monsters, which devoured men and canoes together; that there was even a demon, who was heard from a great distance, who barred the way, and swallowed up all who ventured to approach him; finally that the heat was so excessive In those countries that it would inevitably cause our death.

I thanked them for the good advice that they gave me, but told them that I could not follow it, because the salvation of souls was at stake, for which I would be delighted to give my life; that I scoffed at the alleged demon; that we would easily defend ourselves against those marine monsters; and, moreover, that we would be on our guard to avoid the other dangers with which they threatened us. After making them pray to God, and giving them some instruction, I separated from them. Embarking then in our canoes, we arrived shortly afterward at the bottom of the Bay des Puantz, where our Fathers labor successfully for the conversion of these peoples, over two thousand of whom they have baptized while they have been there.

This bay bears a name which has a meaning not so offensive in the language of the savages; for they call it *la bayë sallée* ["salt bay"] rather than Bay des Puans,—although with them this is almost the same and this is also the name which they give to the sea. This led us to make very careful researches to ascertain whether there were not some salt-water springs in this quarter, as there are among the Hiroquois, but we found none. We conclude, therefore, that this name has been given to it on account of the quantity of mire and mud which is seen there, whence noisome vapors constantly arise, causing the loudest and most continual thunder that I have ever heard.

The bay is about thirty leagues in depth and eight in width at its mouth; it narrows gradually to the bottom, where it is easy to observe a tide which has its regular ebb and flow, almost like that of the sea. This is not the place to inquire whether these are real tides; whether they are due to the wind, or to some other cause; whether there are winds, the precursors of the moon and attached to her suite, which consequently agitate the lake and give it an apparent ebb and flow whenever the moon ascends above the horizon. What I can positively state is, that, when the water is very calm, it is easy to observe it rising and failing according to the course of the moon; although I do not deny that this movement may be caused by very remote winds, which, pressing on the middle of the lake, cause the edges to rise and fall in the manner which is visible to our eyes.

We left this bay to enter the river that discharges into it; it is very beautiful at its mouth, and flows gently; it is full of bustards, ducks, teal and other birds, attracted thither by the wild oats of which they are very fond. But after ascending the river a short distance, it becomes very difficult of passage, on account of both the currents and the sharp rocks, which cut the canoes and the feet of those who are obliged to drag them, especially when the waters are low. Nevertheless, we successfully passed those rapids; and on approaching Machkoutens, the Fire Nation, I had the curiosity to drink the mineral waters of the river that is not far from that village. I also took time to look for a medicinal plant which a savage, who knows its secret, showed to Father Alloues with many ceremonies. Its root is employed to counteract snake-bites, God having been pleased to give this antidote against a poison which is very common in these countries. It is very pungent, and tastes like powder when crushed with the teeth; it must be masticated and placed upon the bite inflicted by the snake. The reptile has so great a horror of it that it even flees from a person who has rubbed himself with it. The plant bears several stalks, a foot high, with rather long leaves; and a white flower which greatly resembles the wallflower. I put some in my canoe, in order to examine it at leisure while we continued to advance toward Maskoutens, where we arrived on the 7th of June.

DESCRIPTION OF THE VILLAGE OF MASKOUTENS; WHAT PASSED THERE BETWEEN THE FATHER AND THE SAVAGES. THE FRENCH BEGIN TO ENTER A NEW AND UNKNOWN COUNTRY, AND ARRIVE AT MISSISIPI.

PART ONE • SECTION THREE

Here we are at Maskoutens. This word may, in Algonquin, mean "the Fire Nation," which, indeed, is the name given to this tribe.

Here is the limit of the discoveries which the French have made, for they have not yet gone any farther.

This village consists of three nations who have gathered there—Miamis, Maskoutens, and Kikabous. The former are the most civil, the most liberal, and the most shapely. They wear two long locks over their ears, which give them a pleasing appearance. They are regarded as warriors, and rarely undertake expeditions without being successful. They are very docile, and listen quietly to what is said to them; and they appeared so eager to hear Father Alloues when he instructed them that they gave him but little rest, even during the night. The Maskoutens and Kikabous are ruder, and seem peasants in comparison with the others. As bark for making cabins is scarce in this country, they use rushes; these serve them for making walls and roofs, but do not afford them much protection against the winds, and still less against the rains when they fall abundantly. The advantage of cabins of this kind is that they make packages of them and easily transport them wherever they wish, while they are hunting.

When I visited them, I was greatly consoled at seeing a handsome cross erected in the middle of the village and adorned with many white skins, red belts, and bows and arrows, which these good people had offered to the Great Manitou (this is the name which they give to God). They did this to thank Him for having had pity on them during the winter, by giving them an abundance of game when they most dreaded famine.

I took pleasure in observing the situation of this village. It is beautiful and very pleasing; for, from an eminence upon which it is placed, one beholds on every side prairies, extending farther than the eye can see, interspersed with groves or with lofty trees. The soil is very fertile, and yields much Indian corn. The Indians gather quantities of plums and grapes, wherewith much wine could be made, if desired.

No sooner had we arrived than we, Monsieur Jollyet and I, assembled the elders together; and he told them that he was sent by Monsieur Our Governor to discover new countries, while I was sent by God to illumine them with the light of the Holy Gospel. He told them that, moreover, the Sovereign Master of our lives wished to be known by all the nations; and that in obeying His will I feared not the death to which I exposed myself in voyages so perilous. He informed them that we needed two guides to show us the way; and we gave them a present, by it asking them to grant us the guides. To this they very civilly consented; and they also spoke to us by means of a present, consisting of a mat to serve us as a bed during the whole of our voyage.

On the following day, the tenth of June, two Miamis who were given as guides embarked with us, in the sight of a great crowd, who could not sufficiently express their astonishment at the sight of seven Frenchmen, alone and in two canoes, daring to undertake so extraordinary and so hazardous an expedition.

We knew that, at three leagues from Maskoutens, was a river which discharged into Missisipi. We knew also that the direction we were to follow in order to reach it was west-southwesterly. But the road is broken by so many swamps and small lakes that it is easy to lose one's way, especially as the river leading thither is so full of wild oats that is difficult to find the channel. For this reason we greatly needed our two guides, who safely conducted us to a portage of 2,700 paces, and helped us to transport our canoes to enter that river; after which they returned home, leaving us alone in this unknown country, in the hands of Providence.

Thus we left the waters flowing to Quebeq, 4 or 500 leagues from here, to float on those that would thenceforward take us through strange lands. Before embarking thereon, we began all together a new devotion to the Blessed Virgin Immaculate, which we practiced daily, addressing to her special prayers to place under her protection both our persons and the success of our voyage; and, after mutually encouraging one another, we entered our canoes.

The river on which we embarked is called Meskousing. It is very wide; it has a sandy bottom, which forms various shoals that render its navigation very difficult. It is full of islands covered with vines. On the banks one sees fertile land, diversified with woods, prairies, and hills. There are oak, walnut, and basswood trees; and another kind, whose branches are armed with long thorns. We saw there neither feathered game nor fish, but many deer and a large number of cattle. Our route lay to the southwest, and, after navigating about 30 leagues, we saw a spot presenting all the appearances of an iron mine; and, in fact, one of our party who had formerly seen such mines, assures us that the one which we found is very good and very rich. It is covered with three feet of good soil, and is quite near a chain of rocks, the base of which is covered by very fine trees. After proceeding 40 leagues on this same route, we arrived at the mouth of our river; and, at 42 and a half degrees of latitude, we safely entered Missisipi on the 17th of June, with a joy that I cannot express.

John Nielson's 1937 portrait of Father Marquette was based on a seventeenth-century portrait.

OF THE GREAT RIVER CALLED MISSISIPI; ITS MOST NOTABLE FEATURES; OF VARIOUS ANIMALS, AND ESPECIALLY THE PISIKIOUS OR WILD CATTLE, THEIR SHAPE AND NATURE; OF THE FIRST VILLAGES OF THE ILINOIS, WHERE THE FRENCH ARRIVED.

PART ONE • SECTION FOUR

Here we are, then, on this so renowned river, all of whose peculiar features I have endeavored to note carefully. The Missisipi River takes its rise in various lakes in the country of the northern nations. It is narrow at the place where Miskous empties; its current, which flows southward, is slow and gentle. To the right is a large chain of very high mountains, and to the left are beautiful lands; in various places, the stream is divided by islands. On sounding, we found ten brasses of water. Its width is very unequal; sometimes it is three-quarters of a league, and sometimes it narrows to three arpents. We gently followed its course, which runs toward the south and southeast, as far as the 42nd degree of latitude. Here we plainly saw that its aspect was completely changed. There are hardly any woods or mountains; the islands are more beautiful, and are covered with finer trees. We saw only deer and cattle, bustards and swans without wings, because they drop their plumage in this country. From time to time, we came upon monstrous fish, one of which struck our canoe with such violence that I thought that it was a great tree, about to break the canoe to pieces. On another occasion, we saw on the water a monster with the head of a tiger, a sharp nose like that of a wildcat, with whiskers and straight, erect ears; the head was gray and the neck quite black; but we saw no more creatures of this sort. When we cast our nets into the water we caught a sturgeon, and a very extraordinary kind of fish. It resembles the trout, with this difference, that its mouth is larger. Near its nose—which is smaller, as are also the eyes—is a large bone shaped like a woman's busk, three fingers wide and cubit long, at the end of which is a disk as wide as one's hand. This frequently causes it to fall backward when it leaps out of the water. When we reached the parallel of 41 degrees 28 minutes, following the same direction, we found that turkeys had taken the place of game; and the *pisikious*, or wild cattle, that of the other animals.

We call them "wild cattle," because they are very similar to our domestic cattle. They are not longer, but are nearly as large again. and more corpulent. When our people killed one, three persons had much difficulty in moving it. The head is very large; the forehead is flat, and a foot and a half wide between the horns, which are exactly like those of our oxen, but black and much larger. Under the neck they have a sort of large dewlap, which hangs down; and on the back is a rather high hump. The whole of the head, the neck, and a portion of the shoulders are covered with a thick mane like that of horses; it forms a crest a foot long, which makes them hideous, and, failing over their eyes, prevents them from seeing what is before them. The remainder of the body is covered with a heavy coat of curly hair, almost like that of our sheep, but much stronger and thicker. It falls off in the summer, and the skin becomes as soft as velvet. At that season, the savages use the hides for making fine robes, which they paint in various colors. The flesh and the fat of the *pisikious* are excellent, and constitute the best dish at feasts. Moreover, they are very fierce; and not a year passes without their killing some savages. When attacked, they catch a man on their horns, if they can, toss him in the air, and then throw him on the ground, after which they trample him under foot, and kill him. If a person fire at them from a distance, with either bow or a gun, he must, immediately after the shot, throw himself down and hide in the grass; for if they perceive him who has fired, they run at him, and attack him. As their legs are thick and rather short, they do not run very fast, as a rule, except when angry. They are scattered about the prairie in herds; I have seen one of 400.

We continued to advance, but, as we knew not whither we were going,—for we had proceeded over one hundred leagues without discovering anything except animals and birds,—we kept well on our guard. On this account, we make only a small fire on land, toward evening, to cook our meals; and, after supper, we remove ourselves as far from it as possible, and pass the night in our canoes, which we anchor in the river at some distance from the shore. This does not prevent us from always posting one of the party as a sentinel, for fear of surprise. Proceeding still in a southerly and south-southwesterly direction, we find ourselves at the parallel of 41 degrees, and as low as 40 degrees and some minutes,—partly southeast and partly southwest, after having advanced over 60 leagues since we entered the river, without discovering anything.

Finally on the 25th of June, we perceived on the water's edge some tracks of men, and a narrow and somewhat beaten path leading to a fine prairie. We stopped to examine it; and, thinking that it was a road which led to some village of savages, we resolved to go and reconnoiter it. We therefore left our two canoes under the guard of our people, strictly charging them not to allow themselves to be surprised, after which Monsieur Jollyet and I undertook this investigation—a rather hazardous one for two men who exposed themselves, alone, to the mercy of a barbarous and unknown people. We silently followed the narrow path, and, after walking about 2 leagues, we discovered a village on the bank of a river, and two others on a hill distant about half a league from the first. Then we heartily commended ourselves to God, and, after imploring His aid, we went farther without being perceived, and approached so near that we could even hear the savages talking. We therefore decided that it was time to reveal ourselves. This we did by shouting with all our energy, and stopped, without advancing any further. On hearing the shout, the savages quickly issued from their cabins. And having probably recognized us as Frenchmen, especially when they saw a black gown,—or, at least, having no cause for distrust, as we were only two men, and had given them notice of our arrival,—they deputed four old men to come and speak to us. Two of these bore tobacco-pipes, finely ornamented and adorned with various feathers. They walked slowly, and raised their pipes toward the sun, seemingly offering them to it to smoke,—without, however, saying a word. They spent a rather long time in covering the short distance between their village and us. Finally, when they had drawn near, they stopped to consider us attentively. I was reassured when I observed these ceremonies, which with them are performed only among friends; and much more so when I saw them clad in cloth, for I judged thereby that they were our allies. I therefore spoke with them first, and asked them who they were. They replied that they were Ilinois; and, as a token of peace, they offered us their pipes to smoke. They afterward invited us to enter their village, where all the people impatiently awaited us. These pipes for smoking tobacco are called in this country calumets. This word has come so much into use that, in order to be understood, I shall be obliged to use it, as I shall often have to mention these pipes.

How THE ILINOIS RECEIVED THE FATHER IN THEIR VILLAGE.

PART ONE • SECTION FIVE

At the door of the cabin in which we were to be received was an old man, who awaited us in a rather surprising attitude, which constitutes a part of the ceremonial that they observe when they receive strangers. This man stood erect, and stark naked, with his hands extended and lifted toward the sun, as if he wished to protect himself from its rays, which nevertheless shone upon his face through his fingers. When we came near him, he paid us this compliment: "How beautiful the sun is, O Frenchman, when thou comest to visit us! All our village awaits thee, and thou shalt enter our cabins in peace." Having said this, he made us enter his own, in which were a crowd of people: they devoured us with their eyes, but, nevertheless, observed profound silence. We could, however, hear these words, which were addressed to us from time to time in a low voice: "How good it is, my brothers, that you should visit us."

After we had taken our places, the usual civility of the country was paid to us, which consisted in offering us the calumet. This must not be refused, unless one wishes to be considered an enemy, or at least uncivil; it suffices that one make a pretense of smoking. While all the elders smoked after us, in order to do us honor, we received an invitation on behalf of the great captain of all the Ilinois to proceed to his village where he wished to hold a council with us. We went thither in a large company, for all these people who had never seen any Frenchmen among them, could not cease looking at us. They lay on the grass along the road; they preceded us, and then retraced their steps to come and see us again. All this was done noiselessly, and with marks of great respect for us.

When we reached the village of the great captain, we saw him at the entrance of his cabin, between two old men,—all three erect and naked, and holding their calumet turned toward the sun. He harangued us in a few words, congratulating us upon our arrival. He afterward offered us his calumet, and made us smoke while we entered his cabin, where we received all their usual kind attentions.

Seeing all assembled and silent, I spoke to them by four presents that I gave them. By the first, I told them that we were journeying peacefully to visit the nations dwelling on the river as far as the sea. By the second, I announced to them that God, who had created them, had pity on them, inasmuch as, after they had so long been ignorant of Him, He wished to make Himself known to all the peoples; that I was sent by Him for that purpose; and that it was for them to acknowledge and obey Him. By the third, I said that the great captain of the French informed them that he it was who restored peace everywhere; and that he had subdued the Iroquois. Finally, by the fourth, we begged them to give us all the information that they had about the sea, and about the nations through whom we must pass to reach it.

When I had finished my speech, the captain arose, and, resting his hand upon the head of a little slave whom he wished to give us, he spoke thus: "I thank thee, Black Gown, and thee, O Frenchman,"—addressing himself to Monsieur Jollyet,—"for having taken so much trouble to come to visit us. Never has the earth been so beautiful, or the sun so bright, as today; never has our river been so calm, or so clear of rocks, which your canoes have removed in passing; never has our tobacco tasted so good, or our corn appeared so fine, as we now see them. Here is my son, whom I give thee to show thee my heart. I beg thee to have pity on me, and on all my nation. It is thou who knowest the Great Spirit who has made us all. It is thou who speakest to Him, and who hearest His word. Beg Him to give me life and health, and to come and dwell with us, in order to make us know Him." Having said this, he placed the little slave near us, and gave us a second present, consisting of an altogether mysterious calumet, upon which they place more value than upon a slave. By this gift, he expressed to us the esteem that he had for Monsieur Our Governor, from the account which we had given of him; and, by a third, he begged us on behalf of all his nation not to go farther, on account of the great dangers to which we exposed ourselves.

I replied that I feared not death, and that I regarded no happiness as greater than that of losing my life for the glory of Him who has made all. This is what these poor people cannot understand.

The council was followed by a great feast, consisting of four dishes, which had to be partaken of in accordance with all their fashions. The first course was a great wooden platter full of *sagamité,*—that is to say, meal of Indian corn boiled in water, and seasoned with fat. The master of ceremonies filled a spoon with *sagamité* three or four times, and put it to my mouth as if I were a little child. He did the same to Monsieur Jollyet. As a second course, he caused a second platter to be brought, on which were three fish. He took some pieces of them, removed the bones therefrom, and, after blowing upon them to cool them he put them in our mouths as one would give food to a bird. For the third course, they brought a large dog, that had just been killed; but, when they learned that we did not eat this meat, they removed it from before us. Finally, the 4th course was a piece of wild ox, the fattest morsels of which were placed in our mouths.

After this feast, we had to go to visit the whole village, which consists of fully 300 cabins. While we walked through the streets, an orator continually harangued to oblige all the people to come to see us without annoying us. Everywhere we were presented with belts, garters, and other articles made of the hair of bears and cattle, dyed red, yellow, and gray. These are all the rarities they possess. As they are of no great value, we did not burden ourselves with them.

We slept in the captain's cabin, and on the following day we took leave of him promising to pass again by his village, within four moons. He conducted us to our canoes, with nearly 600 persons who witnessed our embarkation, giving us every possible manifestation of the joy that our visit had caused them. For my own part, I promised, on bidding them adieu, that I would come the following year, and reside with them to instruct them. But, before quitting the Ilinois country, it is proper that I should relate what I observed of their customs and usages.

Of the character of the Ilinois; of their habits and customs; and of the esteem that they have for the calumet, or tobacco-pipe, and of the dance they perform in its honor.

PART ONE • SECTION SIX

When one speaks the word "Ilinois," it is as if one said in their language,"the men,"—as if the other savages were looked upon by them merely as animals. It must also be admitted that they have an air of humanity which we have not observed in the other nations that we have seen upon our route. The shortness of my stay among them did not allow me to secure all their information that I would have desired; among all their customs, the following is what I have observed.

They are divided into many villages, some of which are quite distant from that of which we speak, which is called Peouarea. This causes some difference in their language, which, on the whole, resembles Allegonquin, so that we easily understood each other. They are of a gentle and tractable disposition; we experienced this in the reception which they gave us. They have several wives, of whom they are extremely jealous; they watch them very closely, and cut off their noses or ears when they misbehave. I saw several women who bore the marks of their misconduct.

Their bodies are shapely; they are active and very skillful with their bows and arrows. They also use guns, which they buy from our savage allies who trade with our French. They use them especially to inspire, through their noise and smoke, terror in their enemies; the latter do not use guns, and have never seen any since they live too far toward the west. They are warlike, and make themselves dreaded by the distant tribes to the south and west, whither they go to procure slaves; these they barter, selling them at a high price to other nations, in exchange for other wares. Those very distant savages against whom they war have no knowledge of Europeans; neither do they know anything of iron, or of copper, and they have only stone knives. When the Ilinois depart to go to war, the whole village must be notified by a loud shout, which is uttered at the doors of their cabins, the night and the morning before their departure. The captains are distinguished from the warriors by wearing red scarves. These are made, with considerable skill, from the hair of bears and wild cattle. They paint their faces with red ocher, great quantities of which are found at a distance of some days' journey from the village. They live by hunting, game being plentiful in that country, and on Indian corn, of which they always have a good crop; consequently, they have never suffered from famine. They also sow beans and melons, which are excellent, especially those that have red seeds. Their squashes are not of the best; they dry them in the sun, to eat during the winter and spring. Their cabins are very large, and are roofed and floored with mats made of rushes. They make all their utensils of wood, and their ladles out of the heads of cattle, whose skulls they know so well how to prepare that they use these ladles with ease for eating their *sagamité*.

They are liberal in cases of illness, and think that the effect of the medicines administered to them is in proportion to the presents given to the physician. Their garments consist only of skins; the women are always clad very modestly and very becomingly, while the men do not take the trouble to cover themselves. I know not through what superstition some Ilinois, as well as some Nadouessi, while still young, assume the garb of women, and retain it throughout their lives. There is some mystery in this, for they never marry and glory in demeaning themselves to do everything that the women do. They go to war, however, but can use only clubs, and not bows and arrows, which are the weapons proper to men. They are present at all the juggleries, and at the solemn dances in honor of the calumet; at these they sing, but must not dance. They are summoned to the councils, and nothing can be decided without their advice. Finally, through their profession of leading an extraordinary life, they pass for manitous,—that is to say, for spirits,—or persons of consequence.

There remains no more, except to speak of the calumet. There is nothing more mysterious or more respected among them. Less honor is paid to the crowns and scepters of kings than the savages bestow upon this. It seems to be the god of peace and of war, the arbiter of life and of death. It has but to be carried upon one's person, and displayed, to enable one to walk safely through the midst of enemies—who, in the hottest of the fight, lay down their arms when it is shown. For that reason, the Ilinois gave me one, to serve as a safeguard among all the nations through whom I had to pass during my voyage. There is a calumet for peace, and one for war, which are distinguished solely by the color of the feathers with which they are adorned; red is a sign of war. They also use it to put an end to their disputes, to strengthen their alliances, and to speak to strangers. It is fashioned from red stone, polished like marble, and bored in such a manner that one end serves as a receptacle for the tobacco, while the other fits into the stem; this is a stick two feet long, as thick as an ordinary cane, and bored through the middle. It is ornamented with the heads and necks of various birds, whose plumage is very beautiful. To these they also add large feathers,—

red, green, and other colors,—wherewith the whole is adorned. They have a great regard for it, because they look upon it as the calumet of the sun; and, in fact, they offer it to the latter to smoke when they wish to obtain a calm, or rain, or fine weather. They scruple to bathe themselves at the beginning of summer, or to eat fresh fruit, until after they have performed the dance, which they do as follows.

The calumet dance, which is very famous among these peoples, is performed solely for important reasons; sometimes to strengthen peace, or to unite themselves for some great war; at other times, for public rejoicing. Sometimes they thus do honor to a nation who are invited to be present; sometimes it is danced at the reception of some important personage, as if they wished to give him the diversion of a ball or a comedy. In winter, the ceremony takes place in a cabin; in summer, in the open fields. When the spot is selected, it is completely surrounded by trees, so that all may sit in the shade afforded by their leaves, in order to be protected from the heat of the sun. A large mat of rushes, painted in various colors, is spread in the middle of the place, and serves as a carpet upon which to place with honor the god of the person who gives the dance; for each has his own god, which they call their manitou. This is a serpent, a bird, or other similar thing, of which they have dreamed while sleeping, and in which they place all their confidence for the success of their war, their fishing, and their hunting. Near this manitou, and at its right, is placed the calumet in honor of which the feast is given; and all around it a sort of trophy is made, and the weapons used by the warriors of those nations are spread, namely: clubs, war-hatchets, bows, quivers, and arrows.

Everything being thus arranged, and the hour of the dance drawing near, those who have been appointed to sing take the most honorable place under the branches; these are the men and women who are gifted with the best voices, and who sing together in perfect harmony. Afterward, all come to take their seats in a circle under the branches; but each one, on arriving, must salute the manitou. This he does by inhaling the smoke, and blowing it from his mouth upon the manitou, as if he were offering to it incense. Everyone, at the outset, takes the calumet in a respectful manner, and, supporting it with both hands, causes it to dance in cadence, keeping good time with the air of the songs. He makes it execute many differing figures; sometimes he shows it to the whole assembly, turning himself from one side to the other. After that, he who is to begin the dance appears in the middle of the assembly, and at once continues this. Sometimes he offers it to the sun, as if he wished the latter to smoke it; sometimes he inclines it toward the earth; again, he makes it spread its wings, as if about to fly; at other times, he puts it near the mouths of those present, that they may smoke. The whole is done in cadence; and this is, as it were, the first scene of the ballet.

The second consists of a combat carried on to the sound of a kind of drum, which succeeds the songs, or even unites with them, harmonizing very well together. The dancer makes a sign to some warrior to come to take the arms which lie upon the mat, and invites him to fight to the sound of the drums. The latter approaches, takes up the bow and arrows, and the war-hatchet, and begins the duel with the other, whose sole defense is the calumet. This spectacle is very pleasing, especially as all is done in cadence; for one attacks, the other defends himself; one strikes blows, the other parries them; one takes to flight, the other pursues; and then he who was fleeing faces about, and causes his adversary to flee. This is done so well—with slow and measured steps, and to the rhythmic sound of the voices and drums—that it might pass for a very fine opening of a ballet in France.

The third scene consists of a lofty discourse, delivered by him who holds the calumet; for, when the combat is ended without bloodshed, he recounts the battles at which he has been present, the victories that he has won, the names of the nations, the places, and the captives whom he has made. And, to reward him, he who presides at the dance makes him a present of a fine robe of beaver skins, or some other article. Then, having received it, he hands the calumet to another, the latter to a third, and so on with all the others, until every one has done his duty; then the president presents the calumet itself to the nation that has been invited to the ceremony, as a token of the everlasting peace that is to exist between the two peoples. Here is one of the songs that they are in the habit of singing. They give it a certain turn which cannot be sufficiently expressed by note, but which nevertheless constitutes all its grace. *Ninahani, ninahani, ninahani, nani ongo.*

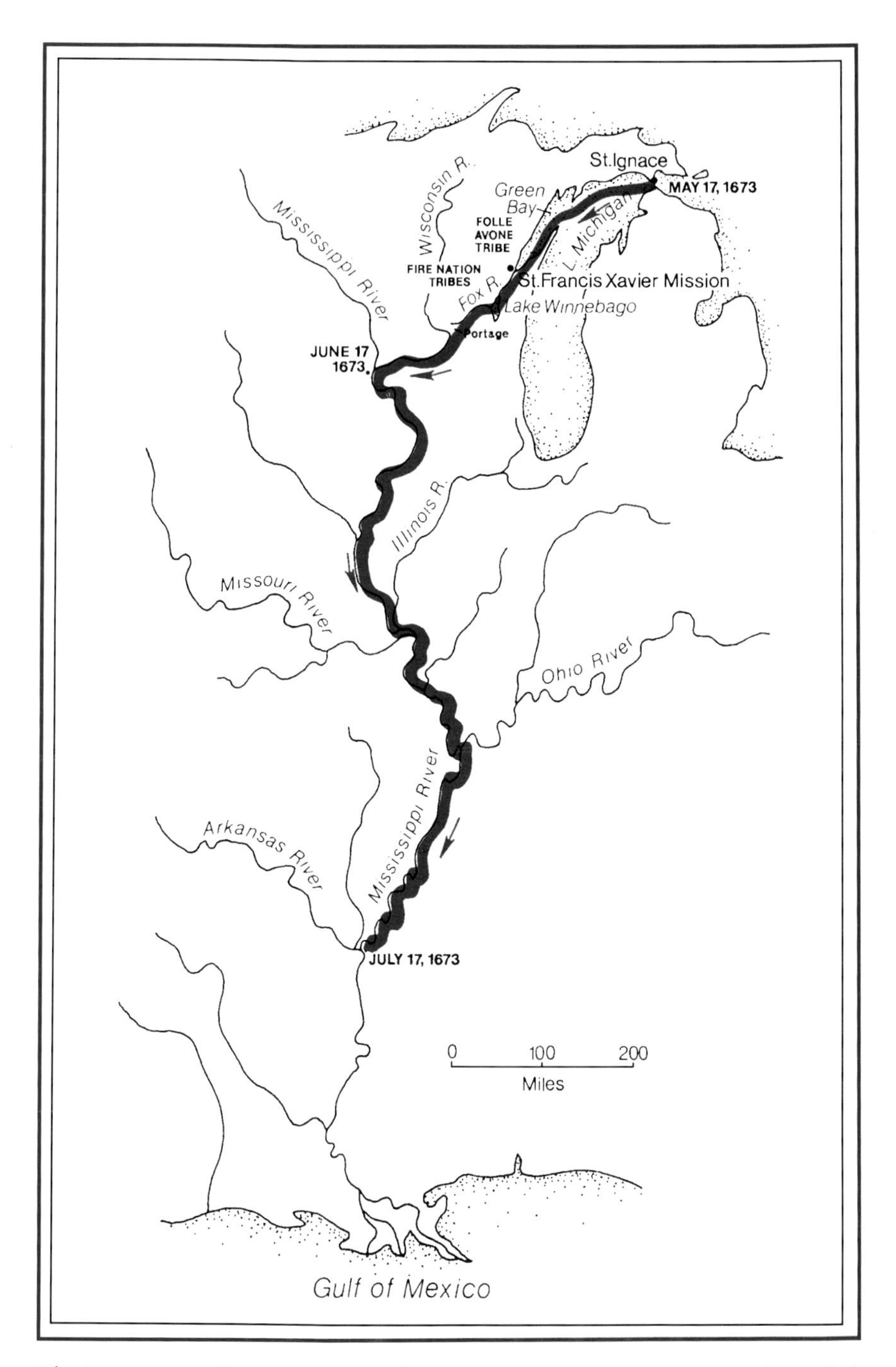

The Marquette-Jolliet expedition left St. Ignace on May 17, 1673, and traveled more than 1,300 miles in two months.

DEPARTURE OF THE FATHER FROM THE ILINOIS; OF THE PAINTED MONSTERS WHICH HE SAW UPON THE GREAT RIVER MISSISIPI; OF THE RIVER PEKITANOUÏ. CONTINUATION OF THE VOYAGE.

PART ONE • SECTION SEVEN

We take leave of our Ilinois at the end of June, about three o'clock in the afternoon. We embark in the sight of all the people, who admire our little canoes, for they have never seen any like them.

We descend, following the current of the river called Pekitanouï, which discharges into the Mississipy, flowing from the northwest. I shall have something important to say about it, when I shall have related all that I observed along this river.

While passing near the rather high rocks that line the river, I noticed a simple which seemed to me very extraordinary. The root is like small turnips fastened together by little filaments, which taste like carrots. From this root springs a leaf as wide as one's hand, and half a finger thick, with spots. From the middle of this leaf spring other leaves, resembling the sconces used for candles in our halls; and each leaf bears five or six yellow flowers shaped like little bells.

We found quantities of mulberries, as large as those of France; and a small fruit which we at first took for olives, but which tasted like oranges; and another fruit as large as a hen's egg. We cut it in halves, and two divisions appeared, in each of which 8 to 10 fruits were encased; these are shaped like almonds, and are very good when ripe. Nevertheless, the tree that bears them has a very bad odor and its leaves resemble those of the walnut-tree. In these prairies there is also a fruit similar to hazelnuts, but more delicate; the leaves are very large, and grow from a stalk at the end of which is a head similar to that of a sunflower, in which all its nuts are regularly arranged. These are very good, both cooked and raw.

While skirting some rocks, which by their height and length inspired awe, we saw upon one of them two painted monsters which at first made us afraid, and upon which the boldest savages dare not long rest their eyes. They are as large as a calf; they have horns on their heads like those of a deer, a horrible look, red eyes, a beard like a tiger's, a face somewhat like a man's, a body covered with scales, and so long a tail that it winds all around the body, passing above the head and going back between the legs, ending in a fish's tail. Green, red and black are the three colors composing the picture. Moreover, these 2 monsters are so well painted that we cannot believe that any savage is their author; for good painters in France would find it difficult to paint so well,—and, besides, they are so high up on the rock that it is difficult to reach that place conveniently to paint them. Here is approximately the shape of these monsters, as we have faithfully copied it.

While conversing about these monsters, sailing quietly in clear and calm water, we heard the noise of a rapid, into which we were about to run. I have seen nothing more dreadful. An accumulation of large and entire trees, branches, and floating islands was issuing from the mouth of the river Pekistanouï, with such impetuosity that we could not without great danger risk passing through it. So great was the agitation that the water was very muddy, and could not become clear.

Pekitanouï is a river of considerable size, coming from the northwest, from a great distance; and it discharges into the Missisipi. There are many villages of savages along this river, and I hope by its means to discover the Vermilion or California Sea.

Judging from the direction of the course of the Missisipi, if it continue the same way, we think that it discharges into the Mexican gulf. It would be a great advantage to find the river leading to the southern sea, toward California; and, as I have said, this is what I hope to do by means of the Pekitanouï, according to the reports made to me by the savages. From them I have learned that, by ascending this river for 5 or 6 days, one reaches a fine prairie, 20 or 30 leagues long. This must be crossed in a northwesterly direction, and it terminates at another small river,-on which one may embark, for it is not very difficult to transport canoes through so fine a country as that prairie. This 2nd river flows toward the southwest for 10 or 15 leagues, after which it enters a lake, small and deep, which flows toward the west, where it falls into the sea. I have hardly any doubt that it is the Vermillion Sea, and I do not despair of discovering It some day, if God grant me the grace and the health to do so, in order that I may preach the Gospel to all the peoples of this new world who have so long groveled in the darkness of infidelity.

Let us resume our route, after escaping as best we could from the dangerous rapid caused by the obstruction which I have mentioned.

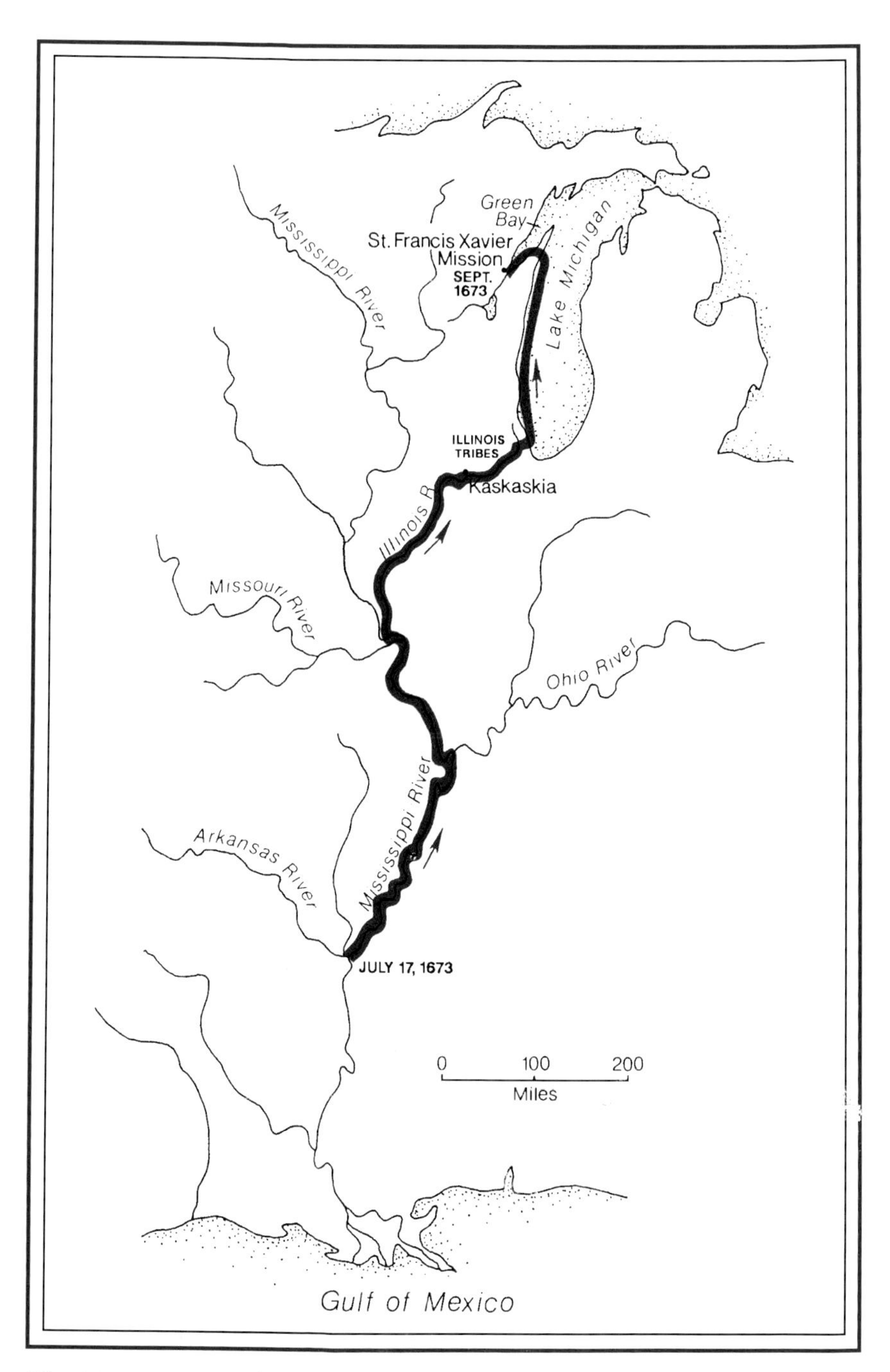

The Marquette expedition traveled 1,140 miles up the Mississippi River to winter camp in Green Bay.

OF THE NEW COUNTRIES DISCOVERED BY THE FATHER. VARIOUS PARTICULARS. MEETING WITH SOME SAVAGES. FIRST NEWS OF THE SEA AND OF EUROPEANS. GREAT DANGER AVOIDED BY MEANS OF THE CALUMET.

PART ONE • SECTION EIGHT

After proceeding about 20 leagues straight to the south, and a little less to the southeast, we found ourselves at a river called Ouaboukigou, the mouth of which is at the 36th degree of latitude. Before reaching it, we passed by a place that is dreaded by the savages, because they believe that a manitou is there,—that is to say, a demon,— that devours travelers; and the savages, who wished to divert us from our undertaking, warned us against it. This is the demon; there is a small cove, surrounded by rocks 20 feet high, into which the whole current of the river rushes; and, being pushed back against the waters following it, and checked by an island near by, the current is compelled to pass through a narrow channel. This is not done without a violent struggle between all these waters, which force one another back, or without a great din, which inspires terror in the savages, who fear everything. But this did not prevent us from passing, and arriving at Waboukigou. This river flows from the lands of the east, where dwell the people called Chaouanons in so great numbers that in one district there are as many as 23 villages, and 15 in another, quite near one another. They are not at all warlike, and are the nations whom the Iroquois go so far to seek, and war against without any reason; and because these poor people cannot defend themselves, they allow themselves to be captured and taken like flocks of sheep; and, innocent though they are, they nevertheless sometimes experience the barbarity of the Iroquois, who cruelly burn them.

A short distance above the river of which I have just spoken are cliffs, on which our Frenchmen noticed an iron mine, which they consider very rich. There are several veins of ore, and a bed a foot thick, and one sees large masses of it united with pebbles. A sticky earth is found there, of three different colors—purple, violet, and red. The water in which the latter is washed assumes a bloody tinge. There is also very heavy red sand. I placed some on a paddle, which was dyed with its color—so deeply that the water could not wash it away during the 15 days while I used it for paddling.

Here we began to see canes, or large reeds, which grow on the banks of the river; their color is a very pleasing green; all the nodes are marked by a crown of long, narrow, pointed leaves. They are very high, and grow so thickly that the wild cattle have some difficulty in forcing their way through them.

Hitherto, we had not suffered any inconvenience from mosquitoes; but we are entering into their home, as it were. This is what the savages of this quarter do to protect themselves against them. They erect a scaffolding, the floor of which consists only of poles, so that it is open to the air in order that the smoke of the fire made underneath may pass through, and drive away those little creatures, which cannot endure it; the savages lie down upon the poles, over which bark is spread to keep off rain. These scaffoldings also serve them as protection against the excessive and unbearable heat of this country; for they lie in the shade, on the floor below, and thus protect themselves against the sun's rays, enjoying the cool breeze that circulates freely through the scaffolding.

With the same object, we were compelled to erect a sort of cabin on the water, with our sails as a protection against the mosquitoes and the rays of the sun. While drifting down with the current, in this condition, we perceived on land some savages armed with guns, who awaited us.

I at once offered them my plumed calumet, while our Frenchmen prepared for defense, but delayed firing, that the savages might be the first to discharge their guns. I spoke to them in Huron, but they answered me by a word which seemed to me a declaration of war against us. However they were as frightened as we were; and what we took for a signal for a battle was an invitation that they gave us to draw near, that they might give us food. We therefore landed, and entered their cabins, where they offered us meat from wild cattle and bear's grease, with white plums, which are very good. They have guns, hatchets, hoes, knives, beads, and flasks of double glass, in which they put their powder. They wear their hair long, and tattoo their bodies after the Hiroquois fashion. The women wear head-dresses and garments like those of the Huron women. They assured us that we were no more than ten days' journey from the sea; that they bought cloth and all other goods from the Europeans who lived to the east, that these Europeans had rosaries and pictures; that they played upon instruments; that some of them looked like me, and had been received by these savages kindly. Nevertheless, I saw none who seemed to have received any instruction in the faith; I gave them as much as I could, with some medals.

This news animated our courage, and made us paddle with fresh ardor. We thus push forward, and no longer see so many prairies, because both shores of the river are bordered with lofty trees. The cottonwood, elm, and basswood trees there are admirable for their height and thickness. The great numbers of wild cattle, which we heard bellowing, lead us to believe that the prairies are near. We also saw quail on the water's edge. We killed a little parroquet, one half of whose head was red, the other half and the neck was yellow, and the whole body green. We had gone down to near the 33rd degree of latitude having proceeded nearly all the time in a southerly direction, when we perceived a village on the water's edge called Mitchigamea. We had recourse to our patroness and guide, the Blessed Virgin Immaculate; and we greatly needed her assistance, for we heard from afar the savages who were inciting one another to the fray by their continual yells. They were armed with bows, arrows, hatchets, clubs and shields. They prepared to attack us, on both land and water; part of them embarked in great wooden canoes—some to ascend, others to descend the river, in order to intercept us and surround us on all sides. Those who were on land came and went, as if to commence the attack. In fact, some young men threw themselves into the water, to come and seize my canoe; but the current compelled them to return to land. One of them then hurled his club, which passed over without striking us. In vain I showed the calumet, and made them signs that we were not coming to war against them. The alarm continued, and they were already preparing to pierce us with arrows from all sides, when God suddenly touched the hearts of the old men, who were standing at the water's edge. This no doubt happened through the sight of our calumet, which they had not clearly distinguished from afar; but as I did not cease displaying it, they were influenced by it, and checked the ardor of their young men. Two of these elders even,—after casting into our canoe, as if at our feet, their bows and quivers, to reassure us-entered the canoe, and made us approach the shore, whereon we landed, not without fear on our part. At first, we had to speak by signs, because none of them understood the six languages which I spoke. At last, we found an old man who could speak a little Ilinois.

We informed them, by our presents, that we were going to the sea. They understood very well what we wished to say to them, but I know not whether they apprehended what I told them about God, and about matters pertaining to their salvation. This is a seed cast into the ground, which will bear fruit in its time. We obtained no other answer than that we would learn all that we desired at another large village, called Akamsea, which was only 8 or 10 leagues lower down. They offered us *sagamité* and fish, and we passed the night among them, with some anxiety.

Reception given to the French in the last village which they saw. The manners and customs of those savages. Reasons for not going farther.

PART ONE • SECTION NINE

We embarked early on the following day, with our interpreter; a canoe containing ten savages went a short distance ahead of us. When we arrived within half a league of the Akamsea, we saw two canoes coming to meet us. He who commanded stood upright, holding in his hand the calumet, with which he made various signs, according to the custom of the country. He joined us, singing very agreeably, and gave us tobacco to smoke; after that, he offered us *sagamité,* and bread made of Indian corn, of which we ate a little. He then preceded us, after making us a sign to follow him slowly. A place had been prepared for us under the scaffolding of the chief of the warriors: it was clean, and carpeted with fine rush mats. Upon these we were made to sit, having around us the elders, who were nearest to us; after them, the warriors; and, finally, all the common people in a crowd. We fortunately found there a young man who understood Ilinois much better than did the interpreter whom we had brought from Mitchigamea. Through him, I spoke at first to the whole assembly by the usual presents. They admired what I said to them about God and the mysteries of our holy faith. They manifested a great desire to retain me among them, that I might instruct them.

We afterward asked them what they knew about the sea. They replied that we were only ten days' journey from it—we could have covered the distance in 5 days; that they were not acquainted with the nations who dwelt there, because their enemies prevented them from trading with those Europeans; that the hatchets, knives, and beads that we saw were sold to them partly by nations from the east, and partly by an Ilinois village situated at four days' journey from their village westward. They also told us that the savages with guns whom we had met were their enemies, who barred their way to the sea, and prevented them from becoming acquainted with the Europeans, and from carrying on any trade with them; that, moreover, we exposed ourselves to great dangers by going farther, on account of the continual forays of their enemies along the river,-because, as they had guns and were very warlike, we could not without manifest danger proceed down the river, which they constantly occupy.

During this conversation, food was continually brought to us in large wooden platters, consisting sometimes of *sagamité,* sometimes of whole corn, sometimes of a piece of dog's flesh. The entire day was spent in feasting. These people are very obliging and liberal with what they have; but they are wretchedly provided with food, for they dare not go and hunt wild cattle, on account of their enemies. It is true that they have an abundance of Indian corn, which they sow at all seasons. We saw at the same time some that was ripe, some other that had only sprouted, and some again in the milk, so that they sow it three times a year. They cook it in great earthen jars, which are well made. They have also plates of baked earth which they use in various ways. The men go naked, and wear their hair short; they pierce their noses, from which, as well as from their ears, hang beads. The women are clad in wretched skins; they knot their hair in two tresses which they throw behind their ears, and have no ornaments with which to adorn themselves. Their feasts are given without any ceremony. They offer the guests large dishes, from which all eat at discretion and offer what is left to one another. Their language is exceedingly difficult, and I could succeed in pronouncing only a few words notwithstanding all my efforts. Their cabins, which are made of bark, are long and wide; they sleep at the two ends, which are raised two feet above the ground. They keep their corn in large baskets made of canes, or in gourds as large as half-barrels. They know nothing of the beaver. Their wealth consists in the skins of wild cattle. They never see snow in their country, and recognize the winter only through the rains, which there fall more frequently than in summer. We ate no other fruit there than watermelons. If they knew how to till their soil, they would have fruits of all kinds.

In the evening, the elders held a secret council, in regard to the design entertained by some to break our heads and rob us; but the chief put a stop to all these plots. After sending for us, he danced the calumet before us, in the manner I have already described, as a token of our entire safety; and, to relieve us of all fear, he made me a present of it.

Monsieur Jolliet and I held another council, to deliberate upon what we should do—whether we should push on, or remain content with the discovery which we had made. After attentively considering that we were not far from the Gulf of Mexico, the basin of which is at the latitude of 31 degrees 60 minutes, while we were at 33 degrees 40 minutes, we judged that we could not be more than 2 or 3 days' journey from it; and that, beyond a doubt, the Missisipi river discharges into the Florida or Mexican gulf, and not to the east in Virginia, whose sea-coast is at 34 degrees latitude,—which we had passed, without, however, having yet reached the sea,—or to the west in California, because in that case our route would have been to the west, or the west-southwest, whereas we had always continued it toward the south. We further considered that we exposed ourselves to the risk of losing the results of this voyage, of which we could give no information if we proceeded to fling ourselves into the hands of the Spaniards who, without doubt, would at least have detained us as captives. Moreover, we saw very plainly that we were not in a condition to resist savages allied to the Europeans, who were numerous, and expert in firing guns, and who continually infested the lower part of the river. Finally, we had obtained all the information that could be desired in regard to this discovery. All these reasons induced us to decide upon returning; this we announced to the savages and, after a day's rest, made our preparations for it.

RETURN OF THE FATHER AND OF THE FRENCH. BAPTISM OF A DYING CHILD.

PART ONE • SECTION TEN

After a month's navigation, while descending Missisipi from the 42nd to the 34th degree, and beyond, and after preaching the Gospel as well as I could to the nations that I met, we start on the 17th of July from the village of the Akensea, to retrace our steps. We therefore re-ascend the Missisipi which gives us much trouble in breasting its currents. It is true that we leave it, at about the 38th degree, to enter another river, which greatly shortens our road, and takes us with but little effort to the lake of the Ilinois.

We have seen nothing like this river that we enter, as regards its fertility of soil, its prairies and woods; its cattle, elk, deer, wildcats, bustards, swans, ducks, parroquets, and even beaver. There are many small lakes and rivers. That on which we sailed is wide, deep, and still, for 65 leagues. In the spring and during part of the summer there is only one portage of half a league. We found on it a village of Ilinois called Kaskasia, consisting of 74 cabins. They received us very well, and obliged me to promise that I would return to instruct them. One of the chiefs of this nation, with his young men, escorted us to the lake of the Ilinois, whence at last, at the end of September, we reached the Bay des Puantz, from which we had started at the beginning of June.

Had this voyage resulted in the salvation of even one soul, I would consider all my troubles well rewarded, and I have reason to presume that such is the case. For, when I was returning, we passed through the Ilinois of Peouarea, and during three days I preached the faith in all their cabins; after which, while we were embarking, a dying child was brought to me at the water's edge, and I baptized it shortly before it died, through an admirable act of Providence for the salvation of that innocent soul.

Unfinished Journal of Father Jacques Marquette, Addressed to the Reverend Father Claude Dablon, Superior of the Missions.

PART TWO • SECTION ONE

This is Marquette's journal of his second voyage to the Illinois tribes—a journey with a pathetic ending, for he dies on the way, while striving to reach Mackinac. Departing from De Pere, on October 25, 1674, accompanied by two Frenchmen, he enters the waters of Lake Michigan via the portage at Sturgeon Bay. Now begins a long and tedious voyage, so interrupted by storms and severe cold that it is not until December 4 that the party reaches the Chicago River.

My Reverend Father: *Pax Christi.*

Having been compelled to remain at St. Francois throughout the summer on account of an ailment of which I was cured in the month of September, I waited there the return of our people from down below, in order to learn what I was to do with regard to my wintering. They brought me orders to proceed to the mission of La Conception among the Illinois. After complying with Your Reverence's request for copies of my journal concerning the Missisipi River, I departed with Pierre Porteret and Jacque, on the 25th of October, 1674, about noon. The wind compelled us to pass the night at the outlet of the river, where the Poutewatamis were assembling; for the elders would not allow them to go in the direction of the Ilinois, lest the young men, after collecting robes with the goods that they brought from below, and after hunting beaver, might seek to go down in the spring; because they have reason to fear the Nadouessi.

[26th of October] On passing the village, we found only two cabins of savages, who were going to spend the winter at La Gasparde. We learned that 5 canoes of Poutewatamis, and 4 of Ilinois, had started to go to the Kaskaskia.

[27th] We were delayed in the morning by rain; in the afternoon, we had fine, calm weather, so that at Sturgeon Bay we joined the savages, who traveled ahead of us.

[28th] We reached the portage. A canoe that had gone ahead prevented us from killing any game. We began our portage and slept on the other shore, where the stormy weather gave us much trouble. Pierre did not arrive until an hour after dark, having lost his way on a path where he had never been. After the rain and thunder, snow fell.

[29th] Being compelled to change our camping-ground, we continue

to carry our packs. The portage covers nearly a league, and is very difficult in many places. The Ilinois assemble in the evening in our cabin, and ask us not to leave them, as we may need them, and they know the lake better than we do. We promise them this.

[30th] The Ilinois women complete our portage in the morning. We are delayed by the wind. There are no animals.

[31st] We start, with tolerably fair weather, and sleep at a small river. The road by land from Sturgeon Bay is very difficult. Last autumn, we were traveling not far from it when we entered the forest.

[November 1st] After I said Holy Mass, we came for the night to a river, whence one goes to the Poutewatamis by a good road. Chachagwessiou, an Ilinois greatly esteemed among his nation, partly because he engages in the fur trade, arrived at night with a deer on his back, of which he gave us a share.

[2nd] After Holy Mass, we travel all day in very fine weather. We kill two cats, which are almost nothing but fat.

[3rd] While I am ashore, walking on fine sand—the whole water's edge being covered with grass similar to that which is hauled up by the nets at St. Ignace, I come to a river which I am unable to cross. Our people enter it, in order to take me on board; but we are unable to go out, on account of the waves. All the other canoes go on, excepting one, which came with us.

[4th] We are delayed. There seems to be an island out in the lake, for the game go there at night.

[5th] We had considerable difficulty in getting out of the river at noon. We found the savages in a river. where I seized the opportunity of instructing the Ilinois, on account of a feast that Nawaskingwe had just given to a wolfskin.

[6th] We performed a good day's journey. While the savages were hunting, they discovered some tracks of men, and this compelled us to stay over on the following day.

[9th] We landed about 2 o'clock, because there was a good camping ground. We were detained there for 5 days, on account of the great agitation of the lake, although without any wind; and afterward of the snow, which was melted on the following day by the sun, and a breeze from the lake.

[15th] After proceeding a sufficient distance, we camp at a favorable place, where we are detained 3 days. Pierre mends a savage's gun. Snow falls at night, and thaws during the day.

[20th] We sleep near the bluffs, and are very poorly sheltered. The

savages remain behind while we are delayed 2 days and a half by the wind. Pierre goes into the woods, and finds the prairie 20 leagues from the portage. He also goes through a fine canal which is vaulted, as it were, to the height of a man, in which there is water a foot deep.

[23rd] After embarking at noon we experience some difficulty in reaching a river. Then the cold began, and more than a foot of snow covered the ground; it has remained ever since. We were delayed for three days, during which Pierre killed a deer, 3 bustards, and 3 turkeys, which were very good. The others proceeded to the prairies. A savage discovered some cabins, and came to get us. Jacques went there on the following day with him; 2 hunters also came to see me. They were Maskoutens, to the number of 8 or 9 cabins, who had separated from the others in order to obtain subsistence. With fatigues almost impossible to Frenchmen, they travel throughout the winter over very bad roads, the land abounding in streams, small lakes, and swamps. Their cabins are wretched; and they eat or starve, according to the places where they happen to be. Being detained by the wind, we noticed that there were great shoals out in the lake, over which the waves broke continually. Here I had an attack of diarrhoea.

[27th] We had some trouble in getting out of the river; then, after proceeding about 3 leagues, we found the savages, who had killed some cattle, and 3 Ilinois who had come from the village. We were delayed there by a wind from the land, by heavy waves from the lake, and by cold.

[December 1st] We went ahead of the savages so that I might celebrate Holy Mass.

[3rd] After saying Holy Mass, we embarked, and were compelled to make for a point, so that we could land, on account of floating masses of ice.

[4th] We started with a favoring wind, and reached the river of the portage, which was frozen to the depth of half a foot; there was more snow there than elsewhere, as well as more tracks of animals and turkeys.

Navigation on the lake is fairly good from one portage to the other, for there is no crossing to be made, and one can land anywhere, unless one persist in going on when the waves are high and the wind is strong. The land bordering it is of no value, except on the prairies. There are 8 or 10 quite fine rivers. Deer-hunting is very good, as one goes away from the Poutewatamis.

[12th] As we began yesterday to haul our baggage in order to approach the portage, the Ilinois who had left the Poutewatamis arrived, with great difficulty. We were unable to celebrate Holy Mass on

the day of the Conception, owing to the bad weather and cold. During our stay at the entrance of the river, Pierre and Jacques killed 3 cattle and 4 deer, one of which ran some distance with its heart split in 2. We contented ourselves with killing 3 or 4 turkeys, out of the many that came around our cabin because they were almost dying of hunger. Jacques brought in a partridge that he had killed, exactly like those of France except that it had two ruffs, as it were, of 3 or 4 feathers as long as a finger, near the head, covering the 2 sides of the neck where there are no feathers.

[14th] Having encamped near the portage, 2 leagues up the river, we resolved to winter there, as it was impossible to go farther, since we were too much hindered and my ailment did not permit me to give myself much fatigue. Several Ilinois passed yesterday, on their way to carry furs to Nawaskingwe; we gave them one of the cattle and one of the deer that Jacque had killed on the previous day. I do not think that I have ever seen any savages more eager for French tobacco than they. They came and threw beaver-skins at our feet, to get some pieces of it; but we returned these, giving them some pipefuls of the tobacco because we had not yet decided whether we would go farther.

[15th] Chachagwessiou and the other Ilinois left us, to go and join their people and give them the goods that they had brought, in order to obtain their robes. In this they act like the traders, and give hardly any more than do the French. I instructed them before their departure, deferring the holding of a council until the spring, when I should be in their village. They traded us 3 fine robes of ox-skins for a cubit of tobacco; these were very useful to us during the winter. Being thus rid of them, we said the Mass of the Conception. After the 14th, my disease turned into a bloody flux.

[30th] Jacque arrived from the Ilinois village, which is only six leagues from here; there they were suffering from hunger, because the cold and snow prevented them from hunting. Some of them notified La Toupine and the surgeon that we were here; and, as they could not leave their cabin, they had so frightened the savages, believing that we would suffer from hunger if we remained here, that Jacque had much difficulty in preventing 15 young men from coming to carry away all our belongings.

[January 16th, 1675] As soon as the 2 Frenchmen learned that my illness prevented me from going to them the surgeon came here with a savage, to bring us some blueberries and corn. They are only 18 leagues from here, in a fine place for hunting cattle, deer, and turkeys, which are excellent there. They had also collected provisions while waiting for us; and had given the savages to understand that their cabin belonged to the black gown; and it may be said that they have done and said all that could be expected from them. After the surgeon had spent some time here, in order to perform his devotions, I sent Jacque with him to tell the Ilinois near that place that my illness prevented me from going to see them; and that I would even have some difficulty in going there in the spring, if it continued.

[24th] Jacque returned with a sack of corn and other delicacies, which the French had given him for me. He had also brought the tongues and flesh of two cattle, which a savage and he had killed near here. But all the animals feel the bad weather.

[26th] 3 Ilinois brought us, on behalf of the elders, 2 sacks of corn, some dried meat, pumpkins, and 12 beaver-skins; 1st, to make me a mat; 2nd, to ask me for powder; 3rd, that we might not be hungry; 4th, to obtain a few goods. I replied; 1st, that I had come to instruct them, by speaking to them of prayer, etc.; 2nd, that I would give them no powder, because we sought to restore peace everywhere, and I did not wish them to begin war with the muiamis; 3rd, that we feared not hunger; 4th, that I would encourage the French to bring them goods, and that they must give satisfaction to those who were among them for the beads which they had taken as soon as the surgeon started to come here. As they had come a distance of 20 leagues I gave them, in order to reward them for their trouble and for what they had brought me, a hatchet, 2 knives, 3 clasp-knives, 10 brasses of glass beads, and 2 double mirrors, telling them that I would endeavor to go to the village,-for a few days only, if my illness continued. They told me to take courage, and to remain and die in their country and that they had been informed that I would remain there for a long time.

[February 9th] Since we addressed ourselves to the Blessed Virgin Immaculate, and commenced a novena with a Mass,—at which Pierre and Jacque, who do everything they can to relieve me, received Communion—to ask God to restore my health, my bloody flux has left me, and all that remains is a weakness of the stomach. I am beginning to feel much better, and to regain my strength. Out of a cabin of Ilinois, who encamped near us for a month, a portion have again taken the road to the Poutewatamis, and some are still on the lake-shore, where they wait until navigation is open. They bear letters for our Fathers of St. Francois.

[20th] We have had opportunity to observe the tides coming in from

the lake, which rise and fall several times a day; and, although there seems to be no shelter in the lake, we have seen the ice going against the wind. These tides made the water good or bad, because that which flows from above comes from the prairies and small streams. The deer which are plentiful near the lake-shore, are so lean that we had to abandon some of those which we had killed.

[March 23rd] We killed several partridges, only the males of which had ruffs on the neck, the females not having any. These partridges are very good, but not like those of France.

[30th] The north wind delayed the thaw until the 25th of March, when it set in with a south wind. On the very next day, game began to make its appearance. We killed 30 pigeons, which I found better than those down the great river; but they are smaller, both old and young. On the 28th, the ice broke up, and stopped above us. On the 29th, the waters rose so high that we had barely time to decamp as fast as possible, putting our goods in the trees, and trying to sleep on a hillock. The water gained on us nearly all night, but there was a slight freeze, and the water fell a little, while we were near our packages. The barrier has just broken, the ice has drifted away; and, because the water is already rising, we are about to embark to continue our journey.

The Blessed Virgin Immaculate has taken such care of us during our wintering that we have not lacked provisions, and have still remaining a large sack of corn, with some meat and fat. We also lived very pleasantly, for my illness did not prevent me from saying Holy Mass every day. We were unable to keep Lent, except on Fridays and Saturdays.

[31st] We started yesterday and traveled 3 leagues up the river without finding any portage. We hauled our goods probably about half an arpent. Besides this discharge, the river has another one by which we are to go down. The very high lands alone are not flooded. At the place where we are, the water has risen more than 12 feet. This is where we began our portage 18 months ago. Bustards and ducks pass continually; we contented ourselves with 7. The ice, which is drifting down, keeps us here, as we do not know in what condition the lower part of the river is.

[April 1st] As I do not yet know whether I shall remain next summer in the village, on account of my diarrhoea, we leave here part of our goods, those with which we can dispense, and especially a sack of corn. While a strong south wind delays us, we hope to go tomorrow to the place where the French are, at a distance of 15 leagues from here.

[9th] Strong winds and the cold prevent us from proceeding. The two lakes over which we passed are full of bustards, geese, ducks, cranes,

and other game unknown to us. The rapids are quite dangerous in some places. We have just met the surgeon, with a savage who was going up with a canoe-load of furs; but, as the cold is too great for persons who are obliged to drag their canoes in the water, he has made a cache of his beaver-skins, and returns to the village tomorrow with us. If the French procure robes in this country, they do not disrobe the savages, so great are the hardships that must be endured to obtain them.

NARRATIVE OF THE 2ND VOYAGE THAT FATHER MARQUETTE MADE TO THE ILINOIS. HE REACHES THEM, NOTWITHSTANDING HIS ILLNESS, AND BEGINS THE MISSION OF LA CONCEPTION.

PART THREE • SECTION ONE

Father Jacques Marquette, having promised the Ilinois on his first voyage to them, in 1673, that he would return to them the following year, to teach them the mysteries of our religion, had much difficulty in keeping his word. The great hardships of his first voyage had brought upon him a bloody flux, and had so weakened him that he was giving up the hope of undertaking a second. However, his sickness decreased; and, as it had almost entirely abated by the close of the summer in the following year, he obtained the permission of his superiors to return to the Ilinois and there begin that fair mission.

He set out for that purpose, in the month of November of the year 1674, from the Bay des Puants, with two men, one of whom had made the former voyage with him. During a month of navigation on the lake of the Ilinois, he was tolerably well; but, as soon as the snow began to fall, he was again seized with his bloody flux, which compelled him to halt in the river which leads to the Ilinois. It was there that they constructed a cabin in which to pass the winter, amid such inconveniences that, his malady increasing more and more, he saw clearly that God was granting to him the favor which he had so many times besought from Him; and he even told his two companions very plainly that he would certainly die of that malady, and during that voyage. Duly to prepare his soul, despite the severe disposition of his body, he began this so severe winter sojourn by the retreat of St. Ignatius, which he performed with every feeling of devotion, and many celestial consolations; and then he passed the whole of the remaining time in holding Communion with all Heaven,—having, in these deserts, no intercourse with the earth except with his two companions. He confessed them and administered Communion to them twice in the week, and exhorted them as much as his strength permitted him. A short time after Christmas, that he might obtain the favor of not dying without having taken possession of his dear mission, he invited his companions to make a novena in honor of the Immaculate Conception of the Blessed Virgin. His prayer was answered, against all human probability; and his health improving, he prepared himself to go to the village of the Ilinois as soon as navigation should open, which he did with much joy, setting out for that place on the 29th of March. He spent eleven days on the way, during which time he had occasion to suffer much, both from his own illness, from which he had not entirely recovered, and from the very severe and unfavorable weather.

On at last arriving at the village, he was received as an angel from Heaven. After he had assembled at various times the chiefs of the nation, with all the old men, that he might sow in their minds the first seeds of the Gospel, and after having given instruction in the cabins, which were always filled with a great crowd of people, he resolved to address all in public, in a general assembly which he called together in the open air, the cabins being too small to contain all the people. It was a beautiful prairie, close to a village, which was selected for the great council; this was adorned, after the fashion of the country, by covering it with mats and bearskins. Then the Father, having directed them to stretch out upon lines several pieces of Chinese taffeta, attached to these four large pictures of the Blessed Virgin, which were visible on all sides. The audience was composed of 500 chiefs and elders, seated in a circle around the Father, and of all the young men, who remained standing. They numbered more than 1,500 men, without counting the women and children, who are always numerous,—the village being composed of 5 or 600 fires. The Father addressed the whole body of people, and conveyed to them 10 messages, by means of ten presents which he gave them. He explained to them the principal mysteries of our religion, and the purpose that had brought him to their country. Above all, he preached to them Jesus Christ, on the very eve (of that great day) on which he had died upon the cross for them, as well as for all the rest of mankind; then he said Holy Mass. On the third day after, which was Easter Sunday, things being prepared in the same manner as on Thursday, he celebrated the holy mysteries for the 2nd time; and by these two, the only sacrifices ever offered there to God, he took possession of that land in the name of Jesus Christ, and gave to that mission the name of the Immaculate Conception of the Blessed Virgin.

He was listened to by all these peoples with universal joy; and they prayed him with most earnest entreaty to come back to them as soon as possible, since his sickness obliged him to return. The Father, on his side, expressed to them the affection which he felt for them, and the satisfaction that they had given him; and pledged them his word that he, or some other of our Fathers would return to carry on that mission so happily inaugurated. This promise he repeated several times, while parting with them to go upon his way; and he set out with so many tokes of regard on the part of those good peoples that, as a mark of honor they chose to escort him for more than 30 leagues on the road, vying with each other in taking charge of his slender baggage.

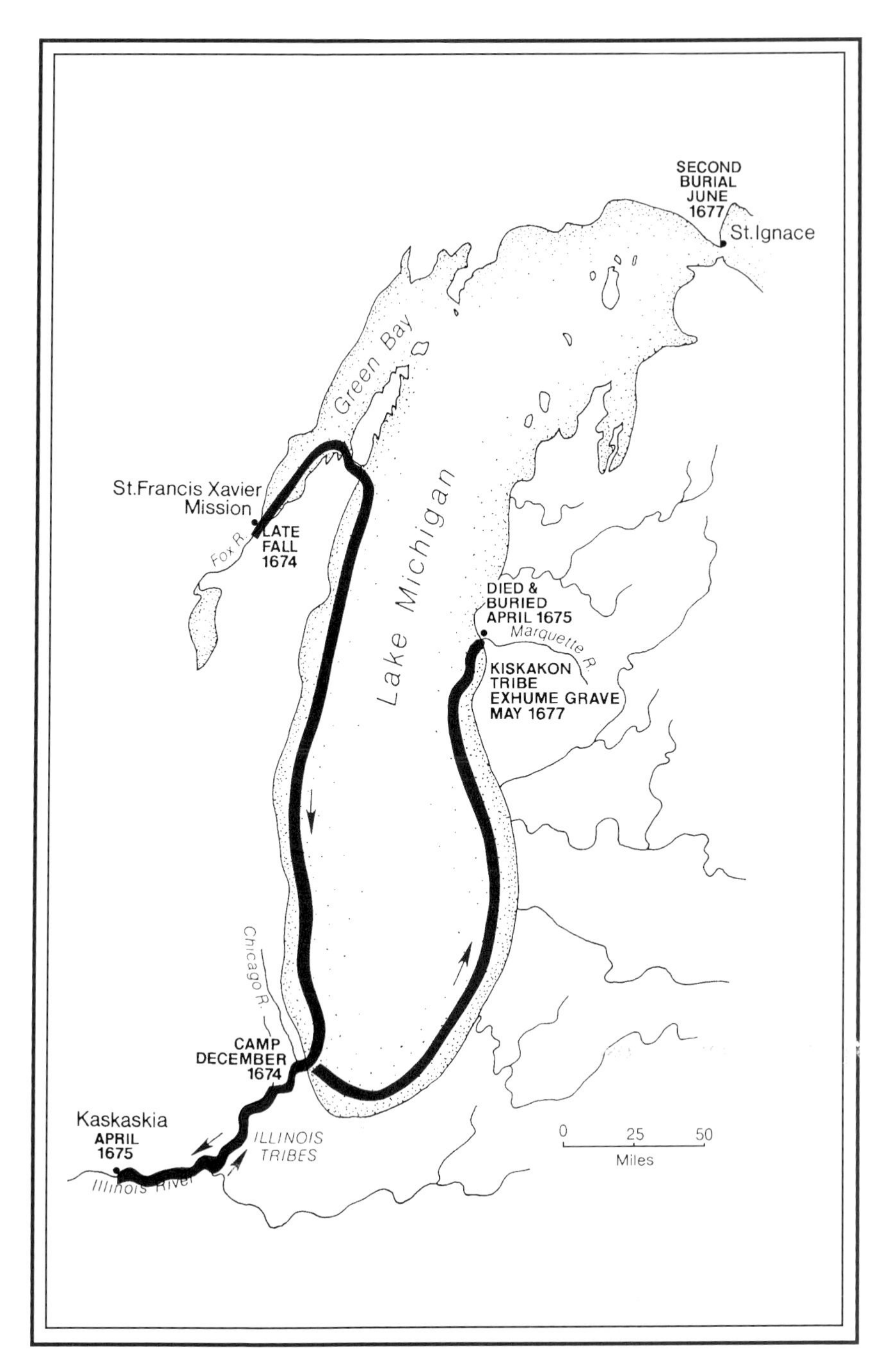

Marquette and two voyageurs traveled 363 miles from Green Bay to visit the Illinois in Kaskaskia. Then they traveled 260 miles to the mouth of the present-day Marquette River where the missionary died and was buried.

THE FATHER IS COMPELLED TO LEAVE HIS ILINOIS MISSION. HIS LAST ILLNESS. HIS PRECIOUS DEATH IN THE HEART OF THE FOREST.

PART THREE • SECTION TWO

After the Ilinois, filled with great esteem for the Gospel, had taken leave of the Father, he continued his journey, and shortly after reached the lake of the Ilinois, upon whose waters he had to journey nearly a hundred leagues, by an unknown route whereon he had never before traveled; for he was obliged to coast along the southern shore of the lake, having come by the northern. But his strength was so rapidly diminishing that his two men despaired of being able to bring him alive to the end of their journey. Indeed, he became so feeble and exhausted that he was unable to assist or even to move himself, and had to be handled and carried about like a child.

Meanwhile, he preserved in that condition an admirable equanimity, resignation, joy, and gentleness, consoling his dear companions and encouraging them to suffer patiently all the hardships of that voyage, in the assurance that God would not abandon them after his death. It was during this voyage that he began to make more special preparation for death. He held Communion, sometimes with our Lord, sometimes with his Holy Mother, or with his guardian angel, or with all Paradise. He was often heard repeating these words: *Credo quod redemptor meus vivit;* or, *maria, mater gratiae, mater dei, memento mei.* In addition to the spiritual exercise, which was read to him every day, he requested toward the close that they would read to him his meditation preparatory for death, which he carried about with him. He recited every day his breviary; and although he was so low that his sight and strength were greatly enfeebled, he continued to do so to the last day of his life, despite the remonstrance of his companions.

Eight days before his death, he was thoughtful enough to prepare the holy water for use during the rest of his illness, in his agony, and at his burial; and he instructed his companions how it should be used.

The evening before his death, which was a Friday, he told them, very joyously that it would take place on the morrow. He conversed with them during the whole day as to what would need to be done for his burial; about the manner in which they should inter him; of the spot that should be chosen for his grave; how his feet, his hands, and his face should be arranged; how they should erect a cross over his grave. He even went so far as to counsel them, 3 hours before he expired, that as soon as he was dead they should take the little hand-bell of his chapel, and sound it while he was being put under ground. He spoke of all these things with so great tranquility and presence of mind that one might have supposed that he was concerned with the death and funeral of some other person, and not with his own.

Thus did he converse with them as they made their way upon the lake,—until, having perceived a river, on the shore of which stood an eminence that he deemed well suited to be the place of his interment, he told them that that was the place of his last repose. They wished, however, to proceed farther, as the weather was favorable, and the day was not far advanced; but God raised a contrary wind, which compelled them to return, and enter the river which the Father had pointed out. They accordingly brought him to the land, lighted a little fire for him, and prepared for him a wretched cabin of bark. They laid him down therein, in the least uncomfortable way that they could; but they were so stricken with sorrow that, as they have since said, they hardly knew what they were doing.

The Father, being thus stretched on the ground in much the same way as was St. Francis Xavier, as he had always so passionately desired, and finding himself alone in the midst of these forests for his companions were occupied with the disembarkation, he had leisure to repeat all the last acts in which he had continued during these last days.

His dear companions having afterward joined him, all disconsolate, he comforted them, and inspired them with the confidence that God would take care of them after his death, in these new and unknown countries. He gave them the last instructions, thanked them for all the charities which they had exercised in his behalf during the whole journey, and entreated pardon for the trouble that he had given them. He charged them to ask pardon for him also, from all our Fathers and brethren who live in the country of the Outaouacs. Then he undertook to prepare them for the sacrament of penance, which he administered to them for the last time. He gave them also a paper on which he had written all his faults since his own last confession, that they might place it in the hands of the Father Superior that the latter might be enabled to pray to God for him in a more special manner. Finally, he promised not to forget them in Paradise; and, as he was very considerate, knowing that they were much fatigued with the hardships of the preceding days, he bade them go and take a little repose. He assured them that his hour was not yet so very near, and that he would awaken them when the time should come as, in fact, 2 or 3 hours afterward he did summon them, being ready to enter into the agony.

They drew near to him, and he embraced them once again, while they burst into tears at his feet. Then he asked for holy water and his reliquary; and having himself removed his crucifix, which he carried always suspended round his neck, he placed it in the hands of one of his companions, begging him to hold it before his eyes. Then, feeling that he had but a short time to live, he made a last effort, clasped his hands, and, with a steady and fond look upon his crucifix, he uttered aloud his profession of faith, and gave thanks to the Divine Majesty for the great favor which He accorded him of dying in the Society, of dying in it as a missionary of Jesus Christ,—and, above all, of dying, as he had always prayed, in a wretched cabin in the midst of the forests and bereft of all human succor.

After that, he was silent, communing within himself with God. Nevertheless he let escape from time to time these words, *Sustinuit anima mea in verbo ejus*; or these, *Mater Dei, memento mei*—which were the last words he uttered before entering his agony, which was, however, very mild and peaceful.

He prayed his companions to put him in mind, when they should see him about to expire, to repeat frequently the names of Jesus and Mary, if he could not himself do so. They did as they were bidden; and, when they believed him to be near his end, one of them called aloud, "Jesus, Mary!" The dying man repeated the words distinctly, several times; and as if, at these sacred names, something presented itself to him, he suddenly raised his eyes above his crucifix, holding them riveted on that object, which he appeared to regard with pleasure. And so, with a countenance beaming and all aglow, he expired without any struggle, and so gently that it might have been regarded as a pleasant sleep.

His two poor companions, shedding many tears over him, composed his body in the manner which he had prescribed to them. Then they carried him devoutly to burial, ringing the while the little bell as he had bidden them; and planted a large cross near his grave, as a sign to passers-by.

When it became a question of embarking, to proceed on their journey, one of the two, who for some days had been so heartsick with sorrow, and so greatly prostrated with an internal malady, that he could no longer eat or breathe except with difficulty, bethought himself, while the other was making all preparations for embarking, to visit the grave of his good Father, and ask his intercession with the glorious Virgin, as he had promised, not doubting in the least that he was in Heaven. He fell, then, upon his knees, made a short prayer, and having reverently taken some earth from the tomb, he pressed it to his breast. Immediately his sickness abated, and his sorrow was changed into a joy which did not forsake him during the remainder of his journey.

What occurred at the removal of the bones of the late Father Marquette, which were taken from his grave on the 19th of May, 1677, the same day as that on which he died in the year 1675. A brief summary of his virtues.

PART THREE • SECTION THREE

God did not permit that a deposit so precious should remain in the midst of the forest, unhonored and forgotten. The savages named Kiskakons, who have been making public profession of Christianity for nearly ten years, and who were instructed by Father Marquette when he lived at the point of St. Esprit, at the extreme of Lake Superior, carried on their last winter's hunting in the vicinity of the lake of the Ilinois. As they were returning in the spring; they were greatly pleased to pass near the grave of their good Father, whom they tenderly love; and God also put it into their hearts to remove his bones and bring them to our church at the mission of St. Ignace at Missilimakinac, where those savages make their abode.

They repaired then, to the spot, and resolved among themselves to act in regard to the Father as they are wont to do toward those for whom they profess great respect. Accordingly, they opened the grave, and uncovered the body; and, although the flesh and internal organs were all dried up, they found it entire, so that not even the skin was in any way injured. This did not prevent them from proceeding to dissect it, as is their custom. They cleansed the bones and exposed them to the sun to dry; then, carefully laying them in a box of birch-bark, they set out to bring them to our mission of St. Ignace.

There were nearly 30 canoes which formed, in excellent order, that funeral procession. There were also a goodly number of Iroquois, who united with our Algonquin savages to lend more honor to the ceremonial. When they drew near our house, Father Nouvel, who is its superior, with Father Piercon, went out to meet them, accompanied by the Frenchmen and savages who were there; and having halted the procession, he put the usual questions to them, to make sure that It was really the Father's body which they were bringing. Before conveying it to land, they intoned the *de profundis* in the presence of the 30 canoes, which were still on the water, and of the people who were on the shore. After that, the body was carried to the church, care being taken to observe all that the ritual appoints in such ceremonies. It remained exposed under the pall, all that day, which was Whitsun-Monday, the 8th of June; and on the morrow, after having rendered to it all the funeral rites, it was lowered into a small vault in the middle of the church, where it rests as the guardian angel of our Outaouas missions. The savages often come to pray over his tomb. Not to mention more than this instance, a young girl, aged 19 or 20 years, whom the late Father had instructed, and who had been baptized in the past year, fell sick, and applied to Father Nouvel to be bled and to take certain remedies. The Father prescribed to her, as sole medicine, to come for 3 days and say a Pater and three Ave's at the tomb of Father Marquette. She did so, and before the 3rd day was cured, without bleeding or any other remedies.

Father Jaques Marquette, of the province of Champagne, died at the age of 38 years, of which 21 were passed in the Society—namely, 12 in France and 9 in Canada. He was sent to the missions of the Upper Algonquins, who are called Outaouacs; and labored therein with the zeal that might be expected from a man who had proposed to himself St. Francis Xavier as the model of his life and death. He resembled that great saint, not only in the variety of barbarian languages which he mastered, but also by the range of his zeal, which made him carry the faith to the ends of this new world, and nearly 800 leagues from here into the forests, where the name of Jesus Christ had never been proclaimed.

He always entreated God that he might end his life in these laborious missions, and that, like his dear St. Xavier, he might die in the midst of the woods bereft of everything. Every day, he interposed for that end both the merits of Jesus Christ and the intercession of the Virgin Immaculate, for whom he entertained a singular tenderness.

Accordingly, he obtained through such powerful mediators that which he solicited with so much earnestness; since he had, like the apostle of the Indies, the happiness to die in a wretched cabin on the shore of Lake Ilinois, forsaken by all the world.

We might say much of the rare virtues of this noble missionary; of his zeal, which prompted him to carry the faith so far, and proclaim the Gospel to so many peoples who were unknown to us; of his gentleness, which rendered him beloved by all, and made him all things to all men—a Frenchman with the French, a Huron with the Hurons, an Algonquin with the Algonquins; of the childlike candor with which he disclosed his heart to his superiors, and even to all kinds of persons, with an ingenuousness which won all hearts; of his angelic chastity; and of his uninterrupted union with God.

But that which apparently predominated was a devotion, altogether rare and singular, to the Blessed Virgin, and particularly toward the mystery of her immaculate conception. It was a pleasure to hear him speak or preach on that subject. All his conversations and letters contained something about the Blessed Virgin Immaculate—for so he always called her. From the age of 9 years, he fasted every Saturday; and from his tenderest youth began to say the little office of the conception, inspiring everyone with the same devotion. Some months before his death, he said every day with his two men a little corona of the immaculate conception which he had devised as follows; after the credo, there is said once the *pater* and *ave*, and then 4 times these words: *Ave filia Dei patris, ave mater filli Dei, ave sponsa spiritus sancti, ave templum totius trinitatis; per sanctam virginitatem et immaculatam conceptionem tuam, purissima virgo, emunda Cor et Carnem meam; in nominee patris, et filii, et spiritus sancti*,—concluding with the *gloria patri*, the whole repeated three times.

He never failed to say the Mass of the Conception,—or, at least, when he could do so, the prayer of the Conception. He hardly meditated upon anything else day and night. That he might leave us an ever-enduring testimony of his sentiments, it was his desire to bestow on the mission of the Ilinois the name of La Conception.

So tender a devotion toward the mother of God merited some singular grace; and she accorded him the favor that he had always requested—to die on a Saturday. His companions never doubted that she appeared to him at the hour of his death, when, after pronouncing the names of Jesus and Mary, he suddenly raised his eyes above his crucifix, holding them fixed on an object which he regarded with extreme pleasure and a joy that showed itself upon his features; and they had at that time, the impression that he had rendered up his soul into the hands of his good mother.

One of the last letters that he wrote to the Father Superior of the missions before his great voyage, is sufficient evidence that such were his sentiments. He begins it thus:

"The Blessed Virgin Immaculate has obtained for me the favor of reaching this place in good health, and with the resolve to correspond to the intentions which God has respecting me, since He has assigned me to the voyage toward the south. I have no other thought than that of doing what God wills. I dread nothing—neither the Nadoissis, nor the reception awaiting me among the nations dismay me. One of two things will happen: either God will punish me for my crimes and cowardice, or else He will give me a share in His cross, which I have not yet carried since my arrival in this country. But this cross has been perhaps obtained for me by the Blessed Virgin Immaculate, or it may be death itself, that I may cease to offend God. It is that for which I try to hold myself in readiness, surrendering myself altogether into His hands. I entreat Your Reverence not to forget me, and to obtain for me of God that I may not remain ungrateful for the favors which He heaps upon me."

There was found among his papers a manuscript entitled "The Directing care of God over a missionary," in which he shows the excellence of that vocation, the advantages which it affords for self-sanctification, and the care that God takes of Gospel laborers. One sees in this little abstract the spirit of God which possessed him.

Selected Bibliography

Jacques Marquette, Joseph S. Donnelly, S. J. Loyola University Press, Chicago, Illinois, 1968.

Marquette's Explorations: The Narratives Reexamined, Raphael N. Hamilton, S. J. The University of Wisconsin Press, Madison, Milwaukee and London, 1970.

The Explorations of Pere Marquette, Jim Kjelgaard. Random House, New York, 1951.

Pere Marquette: Priest, Pioneer and Adventurer, Agnes Ripplier. Doubleday, Doran and Company, Garden City, New York, 1929.

"Father Marquette and Indian Language," George Siebert. Unpublished research paper, 1989.

Father Marquette, Reuben G. Thwaites. D. Appleton and Company, New York, 1902.

The Jesuit Relations and Allied Documents: Travels and Explorations of the Jesuit Missionaries in New France, 1610-1791, Reuben G. Thwaites. Cleveland, 1896-1901.

Acknowledgments

Father Marquette's Journal was produced by the staff of *Michigan History Magazine;* Dr. Roger L. Rosentreter, editor. **Book editor:** Diana Paiz Engle, associate editor, with additional work by Sharon E. McHaney, assistant editor, Paul D. Mehney, editorial assistant and Services for Publishers/Holland. **Introduction:** James H. Schultz, Michigan Historical Museum. **Text file production:** Mary M. Patrick and Mary Jo Remensnyder. **Electronic production:** TypeAlign Inc./Lansing.

Illustration

Front cover: detail from "Jolliet and Marquette," by Robert Thom, ca. 1966, courtesy of Ameritech Michigan's collection of Robert Thom paintings. **Back cover:** Father Marquette monument in Marquette, Michigan by Tom Buchkoe/Marquette. Father Marquette portrait (page 21) courtesy State Archives of Michigan. **Maps:** Sherman Hollander/Okemos.

Father Marquette National Memorial and Museum

From late May through September, visitors of all ages can enjoy a panoramic view of the Mackinac Bridge while learning more about the life of Father Marquette and the Native American cultures he encountered. The National Memorial and Museum—part of the Michigan Historical Museum System—is located in Straits State Park, St. Ignace. A Michigan state parks motor vehicle permit is required for park entry, but the exhibits, audiovisual programs, interpretive trails and annual French Heritage Day celebrations are free of charge. For more information telephone (906) 643-8620.

Michigan History Magazine

One of the nation's leading state history magazines, *Michigan History Magazine* has covered Michigan's fascinating past for more than 80 years. The award-winning bimonthly offers a contemporary and color-filled perspective on history. Look for *Michigan History Magazine*'s 1999 collector's issue devoted to the unique history of the Upper Peninsula. For order and subscription information, telephone (800) 366-3703.